BY PHYLLIS CHESLER

WOMEN AND MADNESS
WOMEN, MONEY AND POWER
ABOUT MEN

ABOUT MEN

by PHYLLIS CHESLER

SIMON AND SCHUSTER
NEW YORK

Published by Simon and Schuster
A Division of Gulf & Western Corporation
Simon & Schuster Building
Rockefeller Center
1230 Avenue of the Americas
New York, New York 10020
Picture editor: Vincent Virga
Designed by Irving Perkins
Manufactured in the United States of America
1 2 3 4 5 6 7 8 9 10

Library of Congress Cataloging in Publication Data

Chesler, Phyllis.
About Men.

Bibliography: p.
1. Men. 2. Sex Role. 3. Fathers and Sons. 4. Men—Psychology.
I. Title.
HQ1067.C43 301.41'1 77-20486

ISBN 0-671-22939-7

The author wishes to thank the following sources for permission to quote material for this book:

AMS Press, Inc., for material from *Eros: The Development of the Sex Relation Through the Ages* by Emil Lucka.

The Associated Press for material from the *New York Post,* copyright © 1967, 1968, 1974, 1975, 1976, 1977 by The Associated Press.

Atheneum, Inc., for material from *A Woman Named Solitude* by André Schwarz-Bart, copyright © 1973 by André Schwarz-Bart.

Basic Books, Inc., for material from "An Analysis of a Phobia in a Five-year-old Boy" in *The Collected Papers of Sigmund Freud,* edited by Ernest Jones, M.D., Volume 3, authorized translation by Alix and James Strachey, published by Basic Books by arrangement with The Hogarth Press, Ltd., and The Institute of Psycho-Analysis, London; and for material from *Sexual Identity Conflict in Children and Adults* by Richard Green, M.D., copyright © 1974 by Richard Green.

Grove Press, Inc., for material from *Last Exit to Brooklyn* by Hubert Selby, Jr., copyright © 1957, 1960, 1961, 1964 by Hubert Selby, Jr.

Harper & Row, Inc., for excerpts from pages 103, 106, 108, with deletions, from "The Root Cause" (first delivered as a lecture under the title "Androgyny") in *Our Blood* by Andrea Dworkin, copyright © 1975 by Andrea Dworkin.

Horizon Press for material from *Women and Their Sexuality in the New Film* by Joan Mellen, copyright © 1974 by Joan Mellen.

International Universities Press, Inc., for material from *Ritual* by Theodor Reik, copyright © 1946 by Theodor Reik.

Les Femmes for material from *Crimes Against Women,* edited by Diana E. H. Russell and Nicole Van de Ven, copyright © 1976 by Diana E. H. Russell and Nicole Van de Ven.

Little, Brown and Company for excerpts from "Color Photos of the Atrocities" in *Color Photos of the Atrocities* by Kenneth Pitchford, copyright © 1970, 1973 by Kenneth Pitchford.

The New York Times for material from *The New York Times,* copyright © 1973, 1974, 1975, 1977 by The New York Times Company.

Princeton University Press for material from Letters 338 J, 343 J, 344 J in *The Freud/Jung Letters: The Correspondence Between Sigmund Freud and C. G. Jung,* edited by William McGuire, translated by Ralph Manheim and R. F. C. Hull, Bollingen Series XCIV, copyright © 1974 by Sigmund Freud Copyrights, Ltd., and Erbengemeinschaft Prof. Dr. C. G. Jung.

Random House, Inc., for excerpts from "The Network of the Imaginary Mother" in *Lady of the Beasts* by Robin Morgan, copyright © 1976 by Robin Morgan; and for material from *The Crowned Cannibals* by Reza Baraheni, copyright © 1977 by Reza Baraheni.

Schocken Books, Inc., for material from *Letter to His Father* by Franz Kafka, copyright © 1953, 1954, 1966 by Schocken Books, Inc.

The Society of Authors on behalf of the Bernard Shaw Estate for material from *Pygmalion* by Bernard Shaw.

Stein & Day Publishers for material from *From Time to Time* by Hannah Tillich, copyright © 1973 by Hannah Tillich.

Times Change Press for material from "Eroticism and Violence in the Father-Son Relationship" by John Stoltenberg in *For Men Against Sexism: A Book of Readings,* edited by Jon Snodgrass, copyright © 1977 by John Stoltenberg.

University of Iowa Press for material from the Introduction by Edwin Honig to *The Nazi Drawings* by Mauricio Lasansky, copyright © 1976 by Edwin Honig.

ACKNOWLEDGMENTS

I thank Elaine Markson for her diplomacy, her patience, and for being there; Vincent Virga for caring enough to get things done—bravely and well; Pat Meehan for her perceptiveness and lightning-quick effectiveness; Joni Evans for her commitment to this work; Alice Mayhew for her very efficient participation; Emily Boxer, Eve Metz and Frank Metz for their warmth, good judgment and careful work.

I thank Barbara Goodstein for her intelligent assistance in art research; Betty Dodson for the generous use of her art books; Laura de Ponte for her sensitivity, humor and loyal secretarial assistance; Jacqui Baker for her excellent typing assistance; the men whom I interviewed; and the men whose books reveal that which still remains hidden.

To Nachmy, who has blessed me with his gentleness and beauty

CONTENTS

PREFACE

Like most women, I've been observing and "interviewing" men all my life—beginning with my father. In writing this book, my questions to men about themselves became more direct. In turn, men often grew uneasy and silent. Wives and mothers whisper of male silence at home—"What is he thinking about?" "Why doesn't he talk to me?" But men are even more skillfully silent upon being questioned by a "strange" woman—by a woman not bound to compassion or secrecy by blood tie or marriage vow.

As a psychologist and an author, I was often perceived as a woman with unnatural authority, or with frightening pretensions to authority. But this was not important if I could still put men at their ease; if I was still able to make men feel nonthreatened and nonjudged; if I could still communicate with men nonverbally, using traditional womanly or feminine body-language signals.

Men's need for maternal compassion and approval is so great, so unconscious, so pervasive, that its shadow fell across every relationship or encounter I've ever had with men. Would I, as a woman, offer this particular man understanding, a sense of importance, a feeling of acceptance? Would I evaluate what a man told me with a Madonna's Pietà-like compassion, with a Magdalene's unquestioning belief?

How well I played the part of mother-woman totally determined how tense, how relieved, how replenished most men, upon being questioned—or involved—felt. Very few men could talk to me without some unconscious reference to this dynamic; very few men could speak freely, or unguardedly, in its definite absence. For this reason, it is almost impossible for a woman's knowledge of men to be "objective" or sterile. Female knowledge of men always partakes of the intimate, the relational, the "subjective."

Upon being questioned about themselves by a woman, many men are reluctant to be tape-recorded, nervous about note-taking, possessive of their information, cautious about revealing anything of themselves. Most of all, men find it startling, absurd, insulting—humorous—to be interviewed *as men:* as part of the "male" condition, as representatives of only one-half of the "human" condition.

Most men are used to asking the questions, used to conducting the interrogation: especially with women. Most adult men are used to knowing the "answers"—or at least used to thinking they should. Unanswered questions from women frustrate, puzzle, and embarrass them. Being interviewed, it is as if they were small boys again, being cross-examined by a mother.

Still, my asking to hear about men from their own lips awakens old longings and habits—in both of us.

After all, men are used to revealing certain things about themselves *only* to women. Most men expect women in general to keep male secrets, cherish male frailty, forgive male cruelty; women in general to assuage male insecurity and loneliness; women in general to provide them with some comfort, some immediate validation of themselves.

Rarely do men unconsciously expect such unconditional compliance from each other. Adult men expect understanding or compliance only from specific, other men (never men in general), and then "contractually," in terms of *mutual* understanding.

It *was* strange to be "interviewing" men—strange men, and in memory, the men I'd lived with, in love or marriage: as if all men had suddenly become total strangers to me, as if I'd discovered that a close family member was a creature from another planet. Apparently, for me, no ideology: not Psychoanalysis, not Marxism, not Existentialism, not Feminism, could sufficiently answer my questions about man's psychological nature.

For a woman, any woman, this discovery, this fearful clarity, is equivalent, psychologically, to men's nineteenth-century discovery that God is dead. Now, for me, man, as woman's God on earth, had been proclaimed dead. And man as human being remained unknown: to himself, certainly, and to me as a woman, in a different way.

I wrote this book in order to understand men.

First, I turned to books already written by men, about men. I found them of limited usefulness. Only some men, mainly poets and novelists, spoke about themselves in a personally authentic voice; only some men wrote about the male condition with an awareness that it is different from the female condition. Consequently, my deepest questions about male psychology were answered best in myth, in fable, in religious writing, and in painting and sculpture.

Since childhood, I have been a believer in the power of painting and sculpture to capture something essential, something essentially nonverbal, about human consciousness. Controversial and painfully repressed truths about human and male psychology are often more easily understood or experienced through pictures.

Some of the photographs in this book are reproductions of popular "masterpieces" whose significance we rarely contemplate. We do not routinely reflect upon the most familiar, the most taken-for-granted images or events in our daily or cultural life. Thus, Michelangelo's *Creation,* which depicts a male Godhead giving life (or birth) to the world's first man, is not usually seen as an expression of the intense male longing to be able to create life and to be reunited with a loving paternal deity—which it clearly is.

In the beginning, I thought that surely I would create a version of *Women and Madness* for men. But books each have their own way. No matter how hard I struggled to turn this book into a straightforward account of male psychology, the artist in me was seduced by images of men: by gaunt patriarchs and golden warriors, by the haunted poets of romantic Europe, by the masters of death in our own century—and by the images of men that I've known in my own life.

Throughout this book, and especially in the Autobiographical Portraits, I have used the naturalness of my female intimacy with men to recall what they revealed to me about their fathers or about their sons; to recall what they revealed to me, in private, about themselves and about other men. These male portraits are character sketches in diary form. They are remembrances of men I have known and loved; remembrances of men who've betrayed me by dying, by ambivalence, by fear, by cruelty . . . and whom I've betrayed in turn, by ceasing to love them, or by never forgiving them their fragility in the face of love.

Thinking about men, I began to rethink the themes of Eden. I became frightened by the silence surrounding the historical and psychological practice of paternal infanticide and cannibalism—and by the practice itself. I have now grown sensitive to a specifically male sense of primal guilt and damnation—a sense not experienced by women in quite the same way. Men, more than women, seem tormented by exile from Paradise and Innocence.

Thinking about men, I became concerned with fathers and sons. How do sons relate to their fathers? What do fathers feel about what they most desire, and most fear: their genetic replacements? How does this dynamic ever get resolved? Does it?

We are unused to attributing responsibility to men for how children grow up. It is so much more comfortable to "blame" mothers for anything negative that happens—from male violence and male "schizophrenia," to female "promiscuity" and female masochism. Our self-righteous, outraged tones—in life, and in the psychiatric and psychological literature—are reserved for the facts of *maternal* child abuse. Somehow we find it easier to deny, explain away, or at least "understand" *paternal* child abuse, in terms of "unemployment stress" or male biologically based "short tempers."

However, I knew that father-son hostility and paternal child abuse, like rape, incest, and wife beating, exist. I knew it after listening to men speak about it, after reading the limited studies available on it, and of course, after reading about it for years in sensationalistic newspaper accounts of ghetto or suburban tragedies.

My aim in this book, in terms of fathers and sons, was to sketch out the mythic, historical and psychic dimensions of contemporary mass male-male relationships, a history that includes infanticide, homicide, and full-scale warfare; a history that is recapitulated psychologically in many father-son relationships.

Of course, there are "good" father-son relationships: of mutual trust, respect and protectiveness. But we hear too little about them in our own lives and much more about them in sentimental Hollywood movies. The point is, we hear even less—too little—about "bad" father-son relationships: in both popular and psychiatric literature. Only after understanding the depth and significance of male-male ambivalence, hostility and homicide can all the exceptions be learned from, and celebrated. Hopefully, it will then become very clear how crucial it is for all men to fully enter the Family of Women and Children, not merely as owners or keepers, but as wise and gentle nurturers.

How sad that men would base an entire civilization on the

principle of paternity, upon male legal ownership of and presumed responsibility for children, and then never really get to know their sons or their daughters very well; never really participate, for whatever reason, in parenting, in daily, intimate fathering. . . .

Thinking about men, I became concerned with how men feel about and treat each other. Does "male bonding" exist? Do men really become friends? Do blood brothers or surrogate brothers experience or practice the ideals of brotherhood?

Despite the many accounts of male-male hostility and competition in ghettos, in corporate board rooms, and on the fields of war, there is this to remember: that men do "bond" in some ways, and that women do not.

In truth, when I hear of a man forgiving another man for injuring him; when I hear of a man redeeming another man's mistakes for him; when I hear of men putting aside their "differences," even temporarily, to gain a common "good"; when I hear of father surrogates teaching and protecting younger male apprentices; when I hear the lovingly insane roar of male spectators for male athletes or "heroes" of any sort; when I hear men praising other men for their good work or goodwill; when I hear men mourning the misfortune of other men—then, then, I burn with shame, I blush with envy. I covet men's sense of their own power, their education, their common sense, their allegiance to self-interest—because it allows them, sometimes, to take those risks and losses that make for solidarity, at whatever price, with others of their own sex.

If men are psychologically powerful—men of any class or in any era—why do so many men need such constant and false assurances of their worth? Why are the supposedly powerful so uneasy? Why, as Virginia Woolf pointed out, do men need women to reflect themselves back to themselves twice as large as they really are?

Clearly, paradoxically, men are consumed by a silent fear of other men. Thinking about men, I became concerned with how frantically submissive men can be—toward *male* tyrants—and how much this fear of autonomy, this refuge in subordination, this deadly love-play between men is practiced—and denied. Like so many women, men conform because they are more terrified by the loneliness and vulnerability of freedom than by the injustice of abitrary dictatorship.

Both men and women follow orders—to their own detriment, to their very deaths—when they are given by male dictators, by father-figures on earth and in Heaven.

True rebellion against a father frightens sons terribly. Sons have just barely begun to overthrow their original parents, their mothers. So I am concerned with displacements of male-male rage and grief onto safe targets, namely away from stronger men, away from envied and feared men, and onto weaker men, onto children, onto women.

I am trying to find a weak place in the unbroken line of male death-worship: the worship of sacrificed or murdered firstborn redeemer-sons; the worship of the next life rather than the celebration of *this,* our earthly life.

The color of the sky over Hiroshima, over Nagasaki—a color I never saw, a color that has shaped my generation's mood. The strange red of that sky. The red color of black children's blood in Birmingham; the red-stained color of My Lai; and the bloodless color of Auschwitz smoke: gray, black, wordless; of Dauchau smoke: gray, black, wordless, across the European sky. All, all these colors have been painted by fathers and sons, by "bonded" and by womb-less men.

How shall I speak of woman's involvement? Woman's complicity in man's battle against himself? Woman's profit from, indifference to, phobic fear of the public or "male" arena, which alone determines the quality of the air her children breathe, the quality of the food her children eat, whether her children will live or die, and certainly the quality of her own and other women's survival. Ah, but this is not a book about women. I will not dwell here overly much upon female vices—although I do look at what happens between mothers and sons: a complicated and often tragic relationship.

Thinking about men, I began to realize the significance that blood has for men as a symbol of violence and death, and not as a symbol of a normal biological event. Consequently, men are irrationally afraid of blood and are especially confused by female blood. Female blood is feared, isolated, punished and, strangely, envied by men. The miraculous blood of childbirth; the tabooed menstrual blood, without which there would be no childbirth.

The savage mockery, the sexual punishment by withdrawal of sexual attention, toward those women who can no longer bear children is partly related to male uterus envy. Once the power of the womb is no longer active, is no longer dangerous, is no longer useful to men, then men can gain some small measure of revenge, men can dare to violate or ignore that which they were forced to court or to trap before. Thus, our tradition of mother-in-law jokes; and the avoidance of "older" women by men, both erotically and spiritually.

The book you are about to read deals with the psychosexual bases of male personality from four different points of view: from a mytho-poetic point of view; from a visual point of view; from an autobiographical point of view; and finally, from a more traditional psychological or psychoanalytic point of view.

I hope that this multidimensional approach to male psychology makes what I'm saying *more* accessible to you, at a deeper level, than a simple linear presentation ever could.

I write this book not as a tyrant over men, and not as a sycophant of men. I write without blinding contempt for men, and without any irrational fear—or worship—of men.

I write with compassion, with sorrow, and in prophecy. I write with despair at the spiritual and physical carnage that surrounds us. I write, always, in the belief that understanding can weaken the worship of death—that has dominated patriarchal consciousness and human action for so long.

PART ONE
MALE IMAGES: REFLECTIONS OF EDEN

Fathers and Sons

Womb-less Men

Mothers and Sons

Phallic Sexuality

Brothers

1. FATHERS AND SONS

Take now thy son, thine only son Isaac, whom thou lovest, and get thee into the land of Moriah; and offer him there for a burnt offering upon one of the mountains which I will tell thee of. . . .

And Abraham stretched forth his hand, and took the knife to slay his son.

And the angel of the Lord called . . . And he said, Lay not thine hand upon the lad, . . . for now I know that thou fearest God, seeing thou hast not withheld thy son, thine only son from me.

Genesis 22:2, 10, 11, 12

Thou shalt not delay to offer the first of thy ripe fruits, and of thy liquors: the firstborn of thy sons shalt thou give unto me.

Exodus 22:29

In his days did Hiel the Bethelite build Jericho: he laid the foundation thereof in Abiram his firstborn, and set up the gates thereof in his youngest son Segub, according to the word of the Lord, which he spake by Joshua the son of Nun.

I Kings 16:34

Will the Lord be pleased with thousands of rams, or with ten thousands of rivers of oil? shall I give my firstborn for my transgression, the fruit of my body for the sin of my soul?

Micah 6:7

Unknown. ***Abraham Sacrificing Isaac***

This mosaic, from a sixth-century synagogue floor in Israel, is wonderfully clear. Little Isaac looks as if he is trying to escape. Despite the widespread custom of sacrificing the firstborn male son to God (or gods) in the Middle East, *this* firstborn child wants to live. In fact, the nonsacrifice of Isaac is the first clear precedent against human sacrifice in the Old Testament.

It is important to note that Isaac is a "miraculous" first and only child, born long after his mother Sarah's childbearing years are over. Yet she, the mother, is not consulted, by man or God, in this matter of her son's death as sacred sacrifice.

The practice of human and child sacrifice is continuously referred to and prohibited throughout the Old Testament: twice in Exodus and quite clearly in Joshua, in Judges, in I and II Kings, in Micah, in Chronicles, in Jeremiah, and in Ezekiel.

HAEMON
Father, I am thine, and thou, in thy wisdom, tracest for me rules which I shall follow.

CREON
Yes, this, my son, should be thy heart's fixed law—in all things to obey thy father's will. He who begets unprofitable children—what shall we say that he hath sown, but troubles for himself, and much triumph for his foes?
Sophocles, *Antigone*

Francisco Goya. *Saturn Devouring His Son*

Goya's painting of father-son cannibalism is ferocious, terrifying, and somehow "unnatural." We are more used to seeing or hearing about mothers, not fathers—Goddess Monsters and not Godfather Monsters—who "devour" their sons.

Saturn, or Cronus, is the legendary Father of all the Greek and Roman gods. Like other legendary fathers, he has been warned that one of his many sons will overthrow him. He proceeds to kill, cannibalize, and devour them all, one by one. Only Zeus—or Jupiter—whose *mother* hides him, survives.

A son's rebellion against the arbitrary rule of mothers is understandable. What is puzzling and tragic, however, is the child's irrational and submissive flight into the arms of a father-god whose ability to tyrannize or "devour" his young son or daughter is as great as, if not greater than, anything a mother can do or has already done. For men to deny being wounded or victimized at all by fathers, by father figures, or by male tyrants, is psychologically dangerous: as dangerous as it is for men to deny the powerful psychic hold that mothers once had—or still have—over them.

Coming to terms with *paternal* ambivalence, hostility, or abandonment is what sons are now doing on a worldwide scale. To resolve this ancient and usually unconscious quarrel—without endangering the survival of the planet—is a major task of the next decade.

For me you took on the enigmatic quality that all tyrants have whose rights are based on their person and not on reason.

I was, after all, weighed down by your mere physical presence. There was I, skinny, weakly, slight; you, strong, tall, broad. I felt a miserable specimen, and what's more, not only in your eyes but in the eyes of the whole world, for you were for me the measure of all things.

What must be considered as heightening the effect is that you were then younger and hence more energetic, and that you were, besides, completely tied to the business, scarcely able to be with me once a day, and therefore made all the more profound an impression on me, never really leveling out into the flatness of habit.

What was always incomprehensible to me was your total lack of feeling for the suffering and shame you could inflict on me with your words and judgements. It was as though you had no notion of your power.

How terrible for me was, for instance, that: "I'll tear you apart like a fish". It was also terrible when you ran around the table, shouting, grabbing at one, obviously not really trying to grab, yet pretending to, and Mother (in the end) had to rescue one, as it seemed. Once again one had, so it seemed to the child, remained alive through your mercy and bore one's life hence forth as an undeserved gift from you.

Franz Kafka, Letter to His Father

I can't dislike you, but I will say this to you: you haven't got long before you are all going to kill yourselves . . . I am only what lives inside each and every one of you . . . My father is the jailhouse. My father is your system . . . I am only what you made me. I am only a reflection of you . . . I have ate out of your garbage cans to stay out of jail. I have wore your second-hand clothes . . . I have done my best to get along in your world and now you want to kill me, and I look at you, and then I say to myself, You want to kill me? *Ha! I'm already dead, have been all my life. I've spent twenty-three years in tombs that you built . . . These children, everything they done, they done for the love of their brother . . .* You expect to break me? Impossible! You broke me years ago. You killed me years ago . . .

Charles Manson, under legal examination. From Vincent Bugliosi and Curt Gentry, *Helter Skelter*

Unknown. ***Majesty***

In *Majesty* we see a Catholic depiction of father-son violence.

The themes of paternal infanticide and cannibalism that I've suggested as an alternate or parallel interpretation of the myth and sin of Eden clearly originate in pagan and Biblical times, but clearly they also initiate and dominate the Christian era.

Jesus Christ, a Jew, God's son on earth, is sacrificed by and to God *willingly,* in an unusual show of adult filial obedience. Christ's ascension signifies a new era of father-son relations, a widespread triumph of patriarchal will and exclusive male responsibility for spiritual and public matters. Christ's purpose is novel: to redeem all men from original sin, to ensure the possibility that all men enter the Kingdom of Heaven.

In churches at communion, Christ's body is again eaten in the wafer, his blood symbolically tasted in the wine. In so familiar and so sanctified a ritual, we are meant to forget the bloodiness of the original deed, the basically high price we pay for our illusion of redemption. Especially, we are meant to forget that a father has killed or allowed a son to be killed.

Goya, in his "black period," portrays a pagan male father-god literally eating, devouring, his son. It is a dreadful and frightening sight. Yet few are filled with nausea and trembling upon entering a church, or upon viewing crucifixion scenes in every museum in the Western world.

NR

Children's bones: lying on temple altars, immured in public buildings, floating down Egyptian rivers, wind-bleached on all the mountaintops of China, Greece, Africa.

The Bible is haunted by the ghost of a missing son, a firstborn son, a most-beloved son: a murdered son. The first son, killed by his father, Adam; the Last Son, sacrificed by his father, God.

"The Fall of Man"—what else could
that be but the eating of the fruits of sexual
"knowledge": children? Did Adam eat his
first son raw, still howling in birth blood?
And was Eve as innocent as Jocasta?

A father who kills his son kills his
own lifeline: a case of the Head that ate
its own Tail. Such a man acts as if he will
live forever, as if he were God—or an
animal. For this, man was doomed to die;
for this, man was doomed to live, knowing he
would die.

Even Abraham had to be taught that
an animal could serve his purpose instead.

The Tree of Male Begats: a remarkable acknowledgment of paternal responsibility, a first, stunning blow dealt the crime of infanticide. A record of the sons who made it.

And Adam lived an hundred and thirty years, and begat a son in his own likeness, after his image; and called his name Seth:

And the days of Adam after he had begotten Seth were eight hundred years.

Genesis 5:3–4

How explicit. How literal. Eight hundred years—hardly forever—but far longer than one hundred and thirty years.

Consider: if it were natural for fathers to care for their sons, they would not need so many laws commanding them to do so. Fathers would not have to be tempted into it by offers of immortality, empire, or God's love.

Paternal infanticide and cannibalism—the most original of sins.

William Blake. ***Nebuchadnezzar***

Blake's painting of the "maddened" King Nebuchadnezzar captures the haunted, damned, and frightened look that I imagine fathers would have after beating or killing a child. It is the male saint as beast; the male King as crazed.

Did Adam look this way? Did Orestes, who murdered his mother, look this way? Are such deadly original sins so unredeemable that men have needed to project Original Sin onto women, sensing that it is not within their psychic powers to live with such guilt; sensing that it is not within their powers to expiate such guilt without the miracle of Christ, without Mary's mercy?

A first child, a son. He who
opens the virgin's womb is the thing
most longed for, the thing most feared.
The reminder of one's own death, a
self-replacement—an extra mouth to
feed.

One son said: "My father never
wished me dead. I am very much like him—
in fact, it was I, all along, who longed
for *his* death."

Enter Oedipus. Exit Laius. How
easily we forget that it was Laius, the father,
who commanded his son's death; how easily we
forget that Oedipus fled his *adopted* home lest
he kill his adopted father; how easily we
forget that Oedipus hesitated to defend himself
against the stranger's attack—the stranger
on the road: his true father.

Even now, when fathers kill their sons—
at home, at war—the psychologists say, "Oh,
but the father really meant to kill his own
father, the child's grandfather. It was only
a case of mistaken Oedipal identity." Young
soldiers lie dead, sent there by commanding
father-figures. How proud, how sad
their fathers are: their fathers who never meant
them any harm.

Freud, the Father of Oedipal interpretation;
Freud, who bequeathed me the net of
opposites in which to catch the truth; Freud,
the son, could no more remember the terror
of father-violence than could Freud, the
father, admit to such deeds.

Only yesterday, I asked a male
psychiatrist to tell me about the male fear of male
violence. He said that *that* wasn't the problem
at all. No, what really frightened him were the
gangs of teenage girls who took up the whole
sidewalk! No, he said, lighting his pipe, it is
women that men fear most of all.

Oh. And slowly I began to understand
that father-wounded sons never recover,
never confess, never remember; slowly, I
began to understand why women can never
satisfy the longing of boys who are love-
starved for their fathers; why women can
never exorcise the grief of men, lured
by their fathers into wanting the impossible:
revenge, reunion, redemption.
God Almighty's benevolent protection:
against other men, against the original
female parent, a magic male amulet, a
son's shield against the rising hot shame
of childhood vulnerability.

William Blake. ***The Soul Reunited with God***

In this extraordinary painting by William Blake, we see one of the rare depictions of a deeply repressed male psychological desire: the reunion of son with father, of man with God.

Blake's *Soul* shows us how male infants raise up their arms in joyous, trusting, expectant submission—usually to mother-figures; here, to *the* father-figure. Is there something less shameful, to men, in the image or in the reality of men submitting to other men? Is it somehow less feared, more noble, to be bested or enslaved by "superior" men—better than it is to be bested by "inferior" woman?

Blake's *Soul* is *the* male notion of transcendence, of spirituality, of redemption, and reunion. There is no woman anywhere. In a sense, this is an extreme representation of the unmet yearnings of mortal sons for immortal and omnipotent father-gods, perhaps because their earthly fathers have failed them so, or because their earthly leaders have failed them so.

To me, the mating is homosexually erotic and is a complete denial of the role of woman as Mother, as Healer: She whom sons would yearn to be reunited with, if they were *allowed* to feel this yearning without fear of father reprisal. Do sons wish to mate with their fathers? Is the shame of their abandonment by fathers so great that the "Oedipal dilemma" can only be "resolved" through prohibited erotic means—and then only in a "spiritual" sense which excludes woman entirely? If so, how cruel the cultural taboo, the cultural disgust, for male homosexuality. And how equally cruel for women is our exclusion from unpunished sexual practices; how cruel is our exclusion from authority in public rituals of spiritual transcendence.

The End of The Song

When a man kills a woman,
he doesn't mean to. Murder, men know,
is an affair between men, an endless
reversible chain of Heroes and Gods,
Kings and Prisoners, Winners and Losers,
Fathers and Sons.

Humiliated sons, forgotten sons,
father-wounded sons: who else would
have invented the Myth of a Virgin
Birth? "My mother would never sleep
with that petty tyrant, with that
ordinary bully, my father." My mother
slept only with my True Father Who Art
in Heaven.

Cesare Ripa. ***Evil Thoughts***

Here, a man is obviously dashing infants to their death, yet this woodcut is entitled *Evil* THOUGHTS. Even when the deed is shown to us so graphically, it is somewhat softened by giving it some other name.

Or, another way of looking at this: if a patriarchal God sacrifices His son, or daughter, it is for the Good of us all. Its purpose is "higher," therefore holy—and somehow not *really* the bloody deed it is.

Stalin, Hitler, Nixon—grandiose,
mediocre, paranoid, humiliated: classic
father-wounded sons. Even more father-
wounded than the men who submit to them.

The battle cries of disinherited
Sons rise up in ghettos and colonies
everywhere: starving, rebel barbarians,
at the gates of the deadly King.

In fury, in hunger, they call for
the Father's sacrifice. They say: Let
us make a new religion—brotherhood—
and if blood must be shed, let it be the
Father's, not the Son's.

The guilt of lamenting Sons and
blinded Fathers is truly insupportable.
It burns, it burrows, it explodes—
like the weapons both men use to rid
themselves of each other's flesh.

The Face of our Earth is half eaten
away by the syphilis of greed; cliffs fall
into the sea, boulders have sprung up where
only yesterday wheat fields grew. Wealthy
men buy gold and move to Brazil, where, they
have been told, the nuclear rays will strike
last.

Boy-children roam my rooftops, leave
smaller children mutilated, dead. What does
a five-year-old corpse understand about
Malcolm's chickens come home to roost? No
more than the large-eyed deer, shot ten times
dead by the man in the flabby plaid shirt
understands. No more than the woman just
raped to death by soldiers understands.

No more than I understand what draws men
to sit together these many centuries, chewing
over each piece of the Primal meal, unable to
relinquish—or recognize—the taste of their
own flesh . . . these deeds of cannibalism, these
famous Last Suppers embroidered in gold thread
on velvet.

Mine is the century of Death. Mine is the century of male-birthed children, precocious with radiation.

Man's Son, Manson, is convinced that he, not Rockefeller, should be King. The Son has come to slay the Father. The Resurrection of the Sacrifice. The Second Coming.

I wonder if the Fates still sit at
their work—or have they left their
tapestry undone, for good: the needle, the
thread, dangling, the whole unraveling?

Domenico del Ghirlandaio. ***An Old Man and His Grandson***

This fifteenth-century grandfather is, in one magnificent prolonged gaze, affectionate, reflective, loving, sad, and openly tender toward his grandson. It is almost a "maternal" gaze: undemanding, self-contained, deeply satisfied, utterly complete.

This grandfather's look is one that little boys rarely see—or remember—on their father's faces. This is a look that many fathers may bestow upon their sons only when they are asleep or only when they are very young.

Unknown. ***Vierge Ouvrante*****—closed**

Like Eve, the Virgin is holding the sphere, the apple, that represents the world—and woman's creative dominion over the world. Unlike Eve, she has redeemed herself by not biting into the apple; unlike Eve, she has redeemed herself by producing a divine male child, a redeemer of other men, whom she holds as prominently in her right hand as she holds the uneaten apple in her left hand.

Unknown. ***Vierge Ouvrante*****—opened.**

The terror of little boys forbidden their mothers, the anguish of womb-less men, the fury of dependency denied. How can men ever vanquish death without womb-men, without fathering children? How can men ever risk genuine intimacy with womb-men—when any one of them can turn into a forbidden Mother? Thus, do graybeards sit, frankly foolish, in the stomachs, in the very wombs, of young virgins: unlovely unicorns, trapped forever. And thus, do Fathers kill their sons: a contemptuous measure of womb-less man's power over the womb.

2. WOMB-LESS MEN

Anonymous. ***The Creation of Eve***

The anonymous medieval illustrator of *The Creation of Eve* gives us the clearest image of the unconscious Creation Myth in most Judeo-Christian minds: that of a white male God who is miraculously creating the first man in a long line of Hebrew son-begetting fathers, and who is also creating the second Hebrew woman. According to myth, Lilith, who ran away from Eden, was the first woman.

Here we see Eve emerging out of a sleeping Adam's body, already genuflecting, already a supplicant, already praying to the patriarchal God who conducts her actual and spiritual birth.

FREUD: *But only women have children.*
HANS: *I'm going to have a little girl. . . .*
FREUD: *You'd like to have a little girl.*
HANS: *Yes, next year I'm going to have one. . . .*
FREUD: *But you can't have a little girl.*
HANS: *Oh yes, boys have girls and girls have boys.*
FREUD: *Boys don't have children. Only women, only Mummies have children.*
HANS: *But why shouldn't I?*

Sigmund Freud, "An Analysis of a Phobia in a Five-year-old Boy"

Couvade is the custom observed among many races that the father of a new-born child lies in a bed for a certain period, eating only prescribed foods, abstaining from severe work and from the chase, etc., while his wife who has just given birth to a child carries on her usual occupation. . . . the idea of a lying-in on the part of the man.

Theodor Reik, *Ritual: Four Psychoanalytic Studies*

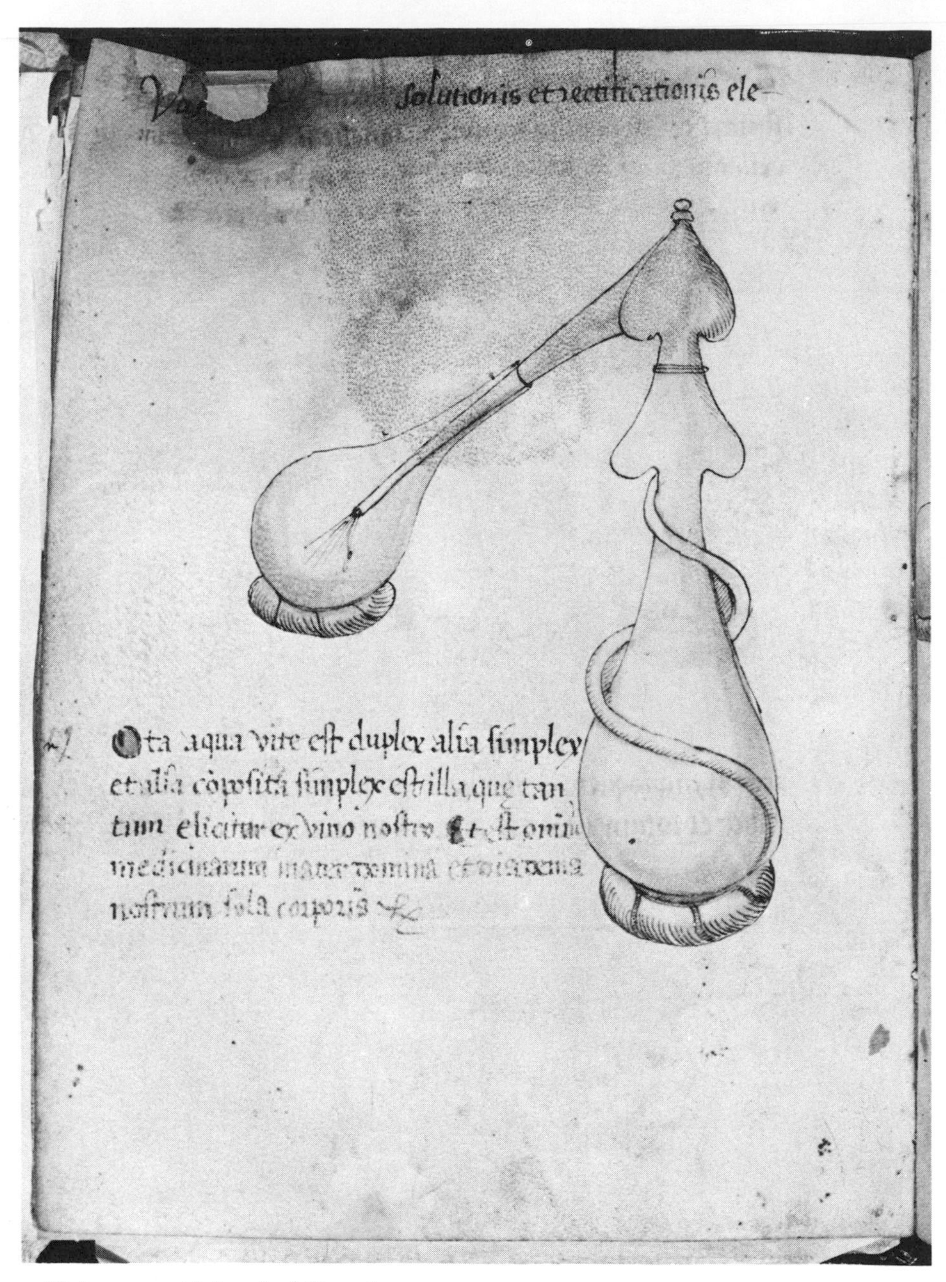

Unknown. ***Alchemical Vessel***

To make something out of "nothing," the way women seem to make new life out of nothing, naturally, effortlessly . . . or so it seems to men. Perhaps men had to invent a mysterious, invisible male sperm-deity to counterbalance the apparent ease with which female deities and/or real women produced children.

Male science, male alchemy, is partially rooted in male uterus envy, in the desire to be able to create something miraculous out of male inventiveness. However, men in science have carried us all to the brink of total planetary, genetic, and human destruction. Repressed and unresolved uterus-envy is a dangerous emotion.

How many men feel the little
man? Longing for a king's riches,
a king's daughter, a woman's birthing
magic? The miller's daughter knows
his name: Rumpelstiltskin, the man
without a womb, the man whose swelling
never lasts nine months, the man who
disappears when his rage is spent.

Haunted and consumed by womb-
envy, men invented alchemy. They
dreamed of spinning something out of
nothing: gold out of straw, new
life out of old life.

Men created civilization in
the image of a perpetual erection: a
pregnant phallus.

Men said: "I have it. In the beginning, there was the Word. I will tell a fabulous lie so often and with such force that everyone will believe it. Soon, no one will even notice the deception."

"Listen, children, here are the facts: Your real Mother is me—your Father!"

It was God, the Father, who gave birth to Adam, and Adam, the man, who gave birth to Eve, and God the Father who Created Christ.

Michelangelo. ***The Creation***
William Blake. ***Elohim Creating Adam***

Michelangelo's *Creation* and William Blake's *Elohim Creating Adam* are both highly artistic expressions of male uterus envy.

Blake, a mystic poet, is depicting a Hebrew event, and is definitively, shockingly erotic in his depiction of the creation of Adam by God. Michelangelo, working out of a classical Greek homosexual tradition, as well as a Catholic anti-woman tradition, is less erotic, more subtle, more muscular, more "spiritual."

Michelangelo's *Creation* is so grand, so exquisite, so compelling, that no one ever wonders: "How can a child be born without a woman being involved? In fact, where is that male God's mother?"

This is the great power of Art and Naming: it blinds us to the simplest, most commonsense truths we know; it allows us, it commands us, to reject our own realities, to reject *ourselves,* in the belief that spiritual perfection is foreign to our personal, mortal consciousness.

Even the pagan male gods gave
birth, but in manly ways—without
losing any blood, without dying.

Zeus gave birth to Athena from
his head, he used his head, he uttered
the Word and she appeared, displaced
upward from the dangerous lower regions
to the lofty regions of the male eye
and ear and brain.

Children, we will go further. We
will circumcise ourselves, and shed blood,
like women. We will make our own vow of
flesh, our own divine covenant with God to
show that we, too, are willing to sacrifice
ourselves in order to perpetuate the race.

Is this why Jews are persecuted—
because, circumcised, they remind all men
of their womb-envy? Or is it for refusing
to believe that one man's sins can be shed
by another man's blood?

Eve's real sin was in mothering Cain, the first man to kill his brother. That Pandora's box could never be closed—no matter how many sacrifice-offerings, circumcisions, and conversions Jewish men performed.

And so men invented Mary, the woman who mothered the first man to redeem all his brothers, Isaac sacrificed, a more universal Joseph, the shedding of sacred male blood, so that it need never be shed again. A grand illusion. A male confusion over maternal blood.

Christian men insisted not on circumcision
but on crucifixion. If female blood
is needed to create human life, then male
blood is needed to divinely *redeem* that human
life. And His side shall be pierced at uterus-
level, and we will worship this male death—
as Eternal Life.

What do women give birth to anyway
but corpses?

God's bosom. In churches, people
sing of it. The milk of our mother's
bosom is God-given, and the way of all
mammals. But man's maternality is a precious
gift, a divine miracle, a freely shouldered
burden: Our Savior's blood.

Poussaint. ***The Judgment of Solomon***

The story of King Solomon's wisdom is not merely a story about a mother's love for her son—a love so great that she would even relinquish him to a female enemy in order that he live—although it is that story too.* More important, it is a story about the patriarchal need to demonstrate that fathers will be better mothers to sons than women are.

Thus, only male judges and male kings, inspired by a male Godhead, can be trusted to save a male child whom a woman might otherwise kill or allow to be killed. Only a male king like King Solomon is able to stop two prostitutes quarreling over an infant son; only a male king can still the vengefulness of women, at least one of whom would have seen a male child torn in two.

This famous tale of Solomon is purposefully deceptive, ironic, and instructive. Throughout the five books of Moses, one of the few "great" deeds allowed the Jewish foremothers was the saving of sons. Moses' mother and his sister Miriam saved him from the Pharaoh's death edict; Jacob's mother Rebekah saved him both from his father Isaac's wrath and from his brother Esau's homicidal fury. Even during Solomon's era, male children were being sacrificed by men to God, or ritually killed to sanctify temple cornerstones.

Yet the power of myth is so great that we remember the "maternal" objectivity and wisdom of Solomon, and the viciousness of women denied ownership of the children they want.

* The female "enemy," by the way, is a woman who has just given birth to a stillborn child, and who was possibly in a state of demented grief when she stole the other woman's newborn child.

Listen, children: The Church is the
true Mother of us all. Naming is all.
Unbaptized, you cannot get into heaven. Only
men in skirts can turn boys into men.

Listen, children: Modern medicine is
the midwife of us all. Science is all.
Only men in aprons can carve up the female
mysteries without risking death.

From behind their veils, from
behind their curtained balconies, the womb-
men, set apart, silently watch this elaborate
procession of velvet and gold: the Majesty
of Couvade.*

The womb-men are content. No longer
need they hide their sons among bulrushes,
among strangers, beneath animal skins or on
the tops of mountains. Now, the womb-less
men, the Fathers, will protect them.

* In orthodox Jewish synagogues, women traditionally sit apart from the men, usually in balconies and often behind screens or curtains, so they will not disturb the men at prayer.

Dressed by her fathers in crimson,
and stiff with silver, she
is borne aloft on their shoulders:
the Daughter of Man. Singing ''Holy, holy,
holy,'' her fathers bring her to the sacred
Ark. Slowly they undress her and, with
great ceremony, spread apart her thighs—
the scrolls of the Torah—and enter the
Kingdom of Queenly Heaven.

High above, the womb-men throw almonds,
raisins, kisses.

Unknown. ***The Tree of Jesse***

Circumcision, Crucifixion, the Kingdom
of Heaven—yet Kings and warriors still
needed blood sisters to shed the only kind of
blood men value: the blood of virgins,
the blood of childbirth.

Peace treaties between men were best
signed in the magic flesh of child brides.

> Show us the blood,
> Show us the child,

and then, we, the grandfathers, the uncles,
the kinsmen, will put our weapons away.

Still, men did not believe
their own ruse. And so they created
money. Horapallo, an ancient
theoretician, proclaimed that

> The scarabeus [is] a
> creature, self-produced,
> being unconceived by a
> female. When the male
> is desirous of procreating,
> he takes the dung
> of an ox and shapes it
> into a spherical form
> like the world.

In Egypt, the world's first coin
was minted in the shape of a scarab beetle.

Money: from scarab beetle to
King's portrait, the coin is sacred
to men. It is men's way of
reproducing and expanding themselves, of
extending their own lifelines.
Priests and Kings had their very own
likenesses engraved on coins: an
endless number of self-reminders, a
genetically metallic miracle.

Money fulfills the alchemists'
desire to turn straw into gold—but
with no need of millers' daughters;
money fulfills the hero's search for
the Golden Fleece—but with no need
of love-starved queens who expect you
to consort with them forever.

Poor King Midas was a dead man without
a woman. Whatever he touched turned to
useless gold—without a King's daughter for
wife, without woman—the connection between
power and ambition, the connection between
king and hero, the connection between father
and son.

Until money invented machines. Now, technological Paradise is within male erotic grasp. Astronauts, both communist and capitalist, lumber on the moon like pregnant women, while scientists on earth try to create life in baby-blue test tubes, the color of death, the color of boys.

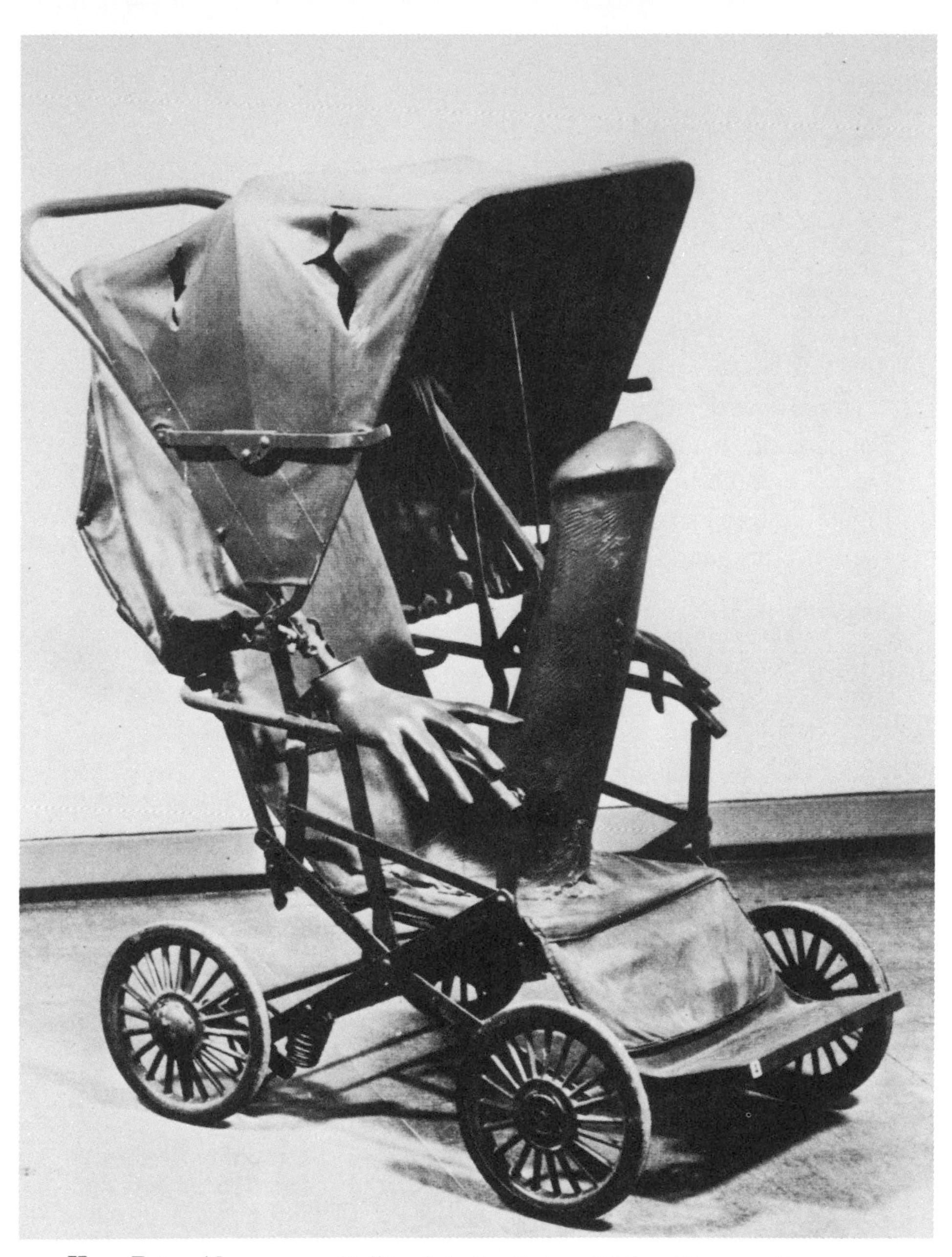

Hans Peter Alvermann. ***Rolling into the Future Without Love or Sorrow***

In this sculpture by the German Alvermann, we see a furiously futurist face of male uterus-envy: not only is Woman as Mother totally absent, but the phallus has even destroyed the object of its uterus-envy. There is no baby in the baby carriage. In its place is a large phallus.

When I see a sculpture like this I am convinced of the dangers of genetic engineering and of test-tube babies. I am reminded of male scientific excesses, which, stemming from uterus-envy, are willing, paradoxically, to sacrifice many people to achieve the larger End.

It is no accident that books of pornographic or erotic art are also the source of many expressions of womb-envy. Dr. Margaret Mead, in a public dialogue with me, noted that "men laugh at sex and women discuss life and death."

In museums, in marble silence, women
are hanging, beautifully clothed and beautifully
naked, painted by great artists who
loved the female body. Strange, how few of
them are pregnant.

Jean Léon Gérôme. *Pygmalion and His Statue*

According to myth, the sculptor Pygmalion lived on the island of Cyprus. He was devoted to his art, and despised the "sexually wanton" women among whom he lived. Pygmalion was a misanthrope who talked to no one and made perfect sculptures. Once he made an ivory statue of a woman so "beautiful" that he fell in love with it. The Goddess Aphrodite, after turning the "sexually wanton" women into rocks, took pity upon Pygmalion and, as he was embracing the cold ivory flesh of his statue, Aphrodite turned her into a *live* or living statue.

How far removed in significance is this from the creation by men of robot-zombies as "perfect wives"—as in the recent Hollywood film *The Stepford Wives?* Or the transformation of Eliza Doolittle by Professor Higgins in *My Fair Lady,* a musical based on G. B. Shaw's dramatization of the Pygmalion myth?

The mindless and joyful prominence this excellent musical has enjoyed in America suggests that men needed to be reminded that, despite the post World War II baby proliferation, *they* alone would make or *try* to make women's reproductions "perfect"—especially to suit their own cantankerous and bachelor-like needs!

3. MOTHERS AND SONS

Unknown. ***Cast of the Venus of Willendorf***
Hans Bellmer. ***Doll***

The *Venus of Willendorf* is one of the oldest discovered Mother Goddess or fertility goddess figurines. It is dated roughly 23,000 B.C. In the twentieth century Hans Bellmer, in his sculpture entitled *Doll*, shows us what became of the Original Venus-Mother. She is now called

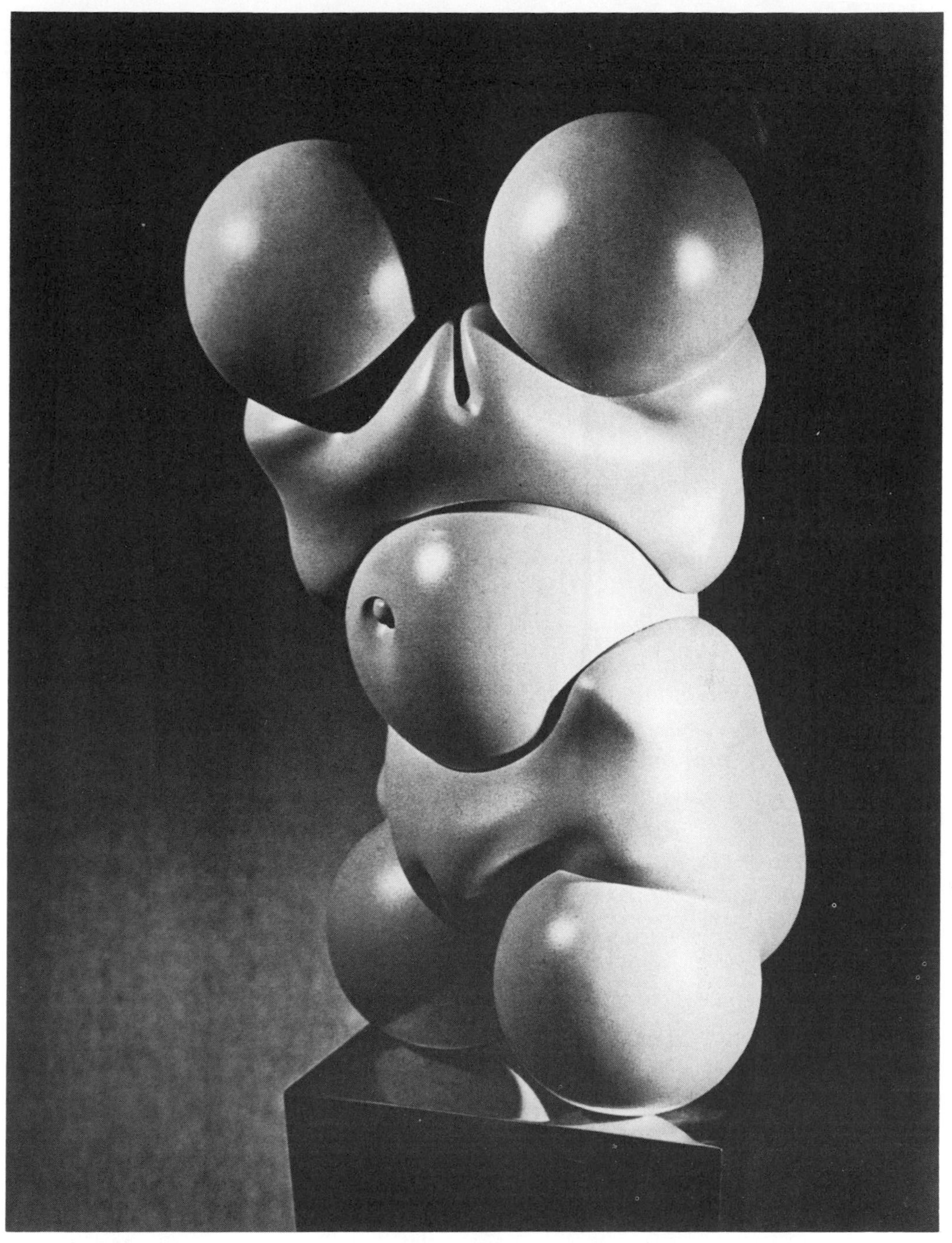

"Doll." Her breasts are hoisted to a shiny breaking point. They are not the breasts of a nursing woman. She is a headless torso, unable to walk—not by time's exigencies, but by sculptor's fiat.

Bellmer has done many sculptures and paintings of female torsos, all mutilated, headless, often hanging upside down from trees, in crucifixion poses, often with virginal bobby socks and patent leather sandals on their feet.

. . . the 10 or 15 drunks dragged Tralala to a wrecked car in the lot on the corner of 57th street and yanked her clothes off and pushed her inside and a few guys fought to see who would be first and finally a sort of line was formed everyone yelling and laughing . . . and more came maybe 40 maybe 50 and they screwed her and went back on line and had a beer and yelled and laughed and someone yelled that the car stunk of cunt so Tralala and the seat was taken out of the car and laid in the lot and she lay there naked on the seat . . . and she drank flipping her tits with the other hand and they all laughed and Tralala cursed and spit out a piece of tooth and they laughed and yelled and the next one mounted her and her lips were split this time and the blood trickled to her chin and someone mopped her brow with a beer soaked handkerchief and another can of beer was handed to her and she drank and yelled about her tits and another tooth was chipped and the split in her lips was widened and everyone laughed and she laughed and she drank more and more and soon she passed out and they slapped her a few times and she mumbled and turned her head but they couldn't revive her so they continued to fuck her as she lay unconscious on the seat in the lot and soon they tired of the dead piece and the daisy-chain broke up . . . and the kids who were watching and waiting to take a turn took out their disappointment on Tralala and tore her clothes to small scraps put out a few cigarettes on her nipples pissed on her jerked-off on her jammed a broomstick up her snatch then bored they left her lying amongst the broken bottles rusty cans and rubble of the lot and Jack and Fred and Ruthy and Annie stumbled into a cab still laughing and they leaned toward the window as they passed the lot and got a good look at Tralala lying naked covered with blood urine and semen and a small blot forming on the seat between her legs as blood seeped from her crotch . . .

Hubert Selby, Jr., "Tralala,"
Last Exit to Brooklyn

What have they done to you?

Barbara Gobel, described by her jailors
as "the fairest maid in Wurzburg,"
burned 1629, age nineteen.
Frau Peller, raped by Inquisition torturers
because her sister refused
the witch-judge Franz Buirman, 1631.

What have they done to me?

Sister Maria Renata Sanger, sub-prioress
of the Premonstratensian Convent of Unter-Zell,
accused of being a lesbian;
the document certifying her torture
is inscribed with the seal of the Jesuits,
and the words Ad Majorem Dei Gloriam—
To the Greater Glory of God.

What have they done to us?

Emerzianne Pichler, tortured and burned together
with her two young children, 1679.
Agnes Wobster, drowned while her small son was forced
to watch her trial by water, 1567.
Veronica Zerritsch, compelled to dance
in the warm ashes of her executed mother,
then burned alive herself, 1754,
thirteen years old.
Frau Dumler, boiled to death in hot oil
while pregnant, 1630.

What have they done?

Robin Morgan, excerpts from "The Network of the Imaginary Mother," *Lady of the Beasts*

Mariko Sato (age 25): Stabbed, hacked and shot. Her body was stripped from the waist down, wrapped in a blanket and stuffed in a trunk in a San Francisco apartment.

Lucy Ann Gilbride (age 52): Slashed and clubbed to death in her home in San Rafael.

Cassie Riley (age 13): Beaten, stripped, raped, drowned, Union City.

Mary E. Robinson (age 23): Stabbed eighteen times by her boyfriend. "She called me a coward," he said. "She said I was afraid to fight for my rights." San Francisco.

Sonya Johnson (age 4): Raped and clubbed, possibly strangled. She was missing eleven days before her body was found and identified. San Jose.

Arlis Perry (age 19): Stabbed, strangled. Raped with altar candles in a church on the Stanford campus. She had been stripped from the waist down.

Maude Burgess (age 83): Left naked and spread-eagled on her bed, her arms and legs tied with sheets. A pillow slip had been pulled over her head. San Francisco.

Darlene Davenport (age 16): Stripped and hacked to death. Left in a parking lot in Oakland.

Excerpts from section on "Femicide" in *Crimes Against Women: The Proceedings of the International Tribunal,*
Diana E. H. Russell and Nicole Van de Ven, editors.

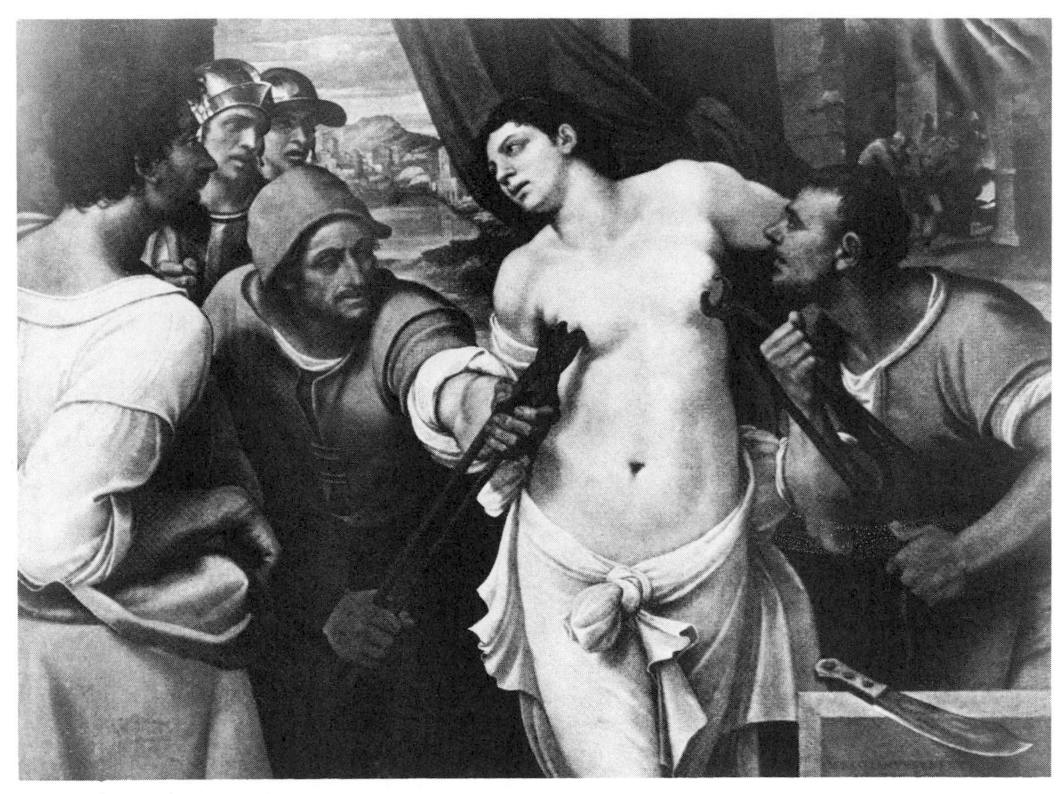

Sebastiano del Piombo. ***The Martyrdom of St. Agatha***

Hell hath no fury like a man spurned. . . . Agatha has been venerated as a third-century virgin martyr, from Catania, Sicily. Legend, which is controversial, has it that Agatha rejected the sexual advances of one Quintian, who then proceeded against her as a Christian. Her tortures included having her breasts cut off—and she is often depicted as carrying her bell-shaped breasts on a dish. Agatha became the patron saint of bell founders.

For those who would like to think that motherhood and the female body are truly cherished, here is a painting, one of the few imaginative "records," shall we say, of the torture and murder of countless millions of women, whether as "Jews," as "Christians," as "witches," or as the captured property of male enemies.

Agatha's breasts—breasts that might ordinarily feed the human race—are being specifically mutilated by men who significantly show little emotion about what they are doing. They are not any more emotionally involved than twentieth-century bomber pilots over Asia are.

What, oh, what, do men want?

Their Mother's Body: Eden's
forbidden fruit. For nine months they
eat of it—and are born guilty. A
son has already mated with his Mother,
a son has already been sheltered and
cradled in the arms of the Tree; a
son is already blinded at birth: by his
mother's blood. The blinding of Oedipus
comes much later—and
needlessly.

A mother's son must avoid all that
floods him with memory of Paradise, and
of Paradise lost.

What, oh, what, do men want?

To forget, to deny, to relive:
the rape, the dismemberment, the murder,
of the original parent. Matricide, not
Patricide, is the primal and still
unacknowledged crime. Father-killing comes
later, and need only happen once, if at
all, to be remembered, regretted, resolved.
Mother-killing must be repeated again and
again and again: expiation for what cannot
be undone.

Mother, mother, why have I forsaken
thee?

Although Magritte's painting entitled *The Rape* has been widely reproduced in books of pornographic or erotic art, I was unable to obtain permission to reproduce it here. No other painting is anywhere as suitable for my purpose. The painting is that of a woman's face and neck.

Thus haunted, men invented the
incest taboo. The erotic maternal:
that ancient Goddess, that dangerous
lover of her son-consort. Hot, hairy,
huge—she is the dragon that sons
must slay in order to become men. It
is the Heroic thing to do.

The incest taboo. The leave-taking
of Mothers, the abandonment of aging wives,
the terror of heterosexual intimacy: the
way in which men learn to murder the object
of their original passion, the way in which
men hide the signs of their first long meal.

The incest taboo. Sex, like
murder, must be committed away from
the Family of Man. Only in foreign
territory must sons learn to strike:
as forcefully as warriors, as mightily
as gods, never exposing their bellies,
never removing their armor. And when
they are captured, sons must give away
as little as possible: sons must deny,
denounce, deceive—and flee in terror,
when they can, from what they most desire.

The many vanishing acts of God and men:
command performances all, an eternity of
enforced escapes, a lonely, manly, wandering.

Edvard Munch. ***Death and the Maiden***

Often, when men embrace women, they report a feeling of suffocation. They flee in terror from the intimacy, they flee in terror from the possibility of becoming a father and of being trapped; they flee equally from the possibility that they will waste their sperm with no gain, no profit, no family security.

Men claim, in the voices of artists, that women represent death, that behind each seductive temptress, behind each virgin daughter of a wealthy father, lies the grinning skull of their own death. Yet I say, as Munch does in this painting, ah, how equally true is the opposite.

How often, how often, have mortal women embraced men and died in childbirth? How often have mortal women embraced men without becoming pregnant, or in becoming pregnant out of wedlock faced the death of social approval and protection? How often have women been forced into involuntary abortions due to poverty or male indifference? How often have women "paid" for the pleasure of children with loneliness, sexual and emotional deprivation, social death?

And how often do women find themselves in the arms of Death upon embracing men? Ghostly embryos and spermlike figures surround Munch's vision of just this Embrace, each floating, disembodied, stillborn—never to be born.

The incest taboo. Have you ever smelled male terror, disguised as moodiness, boredom, anger—as sharply as women do—after sexual intimacy? Have you ever felt how jubilant, how *redeemed,* men sometimes seem, on their way back home from a strange woman? As if they've cheated Death Himself, by so secretly, so quickly, revisiting boyhood's forbidden playmate; by not really revisiting Her at all.

"Other women" are always crude and childish versions of the Original One: cheap, expendable copies thrown from a stranger's mold.

No, sons do not marry their
mothers: older, "wiser," all-powerful,
all-familiar women—as once
their own mothers were to them. Sons
marry wives: "little" mothers, strange
mothers, women safely trapped into
maternal service—hardly the forbidden
breast, hardly the formidable Dragon,
hardly the Tree of Sexual Knowledge,
hardly She who bartered away her freedom
to protect him when he lay swaddled in
vulnerability, exposed to all the elements
of his father's jealousy.

When a wife grows "old"—*as old as his mother once was*—a man must renounce his interest in Her once again. Only the blood of strange women, the blood of ever-younger women, can be pursued without incestuous guilt.

It is redeeming, it is very Biblical, for a man to have sons in his old age.

Salvador Dali. ***Shirley Temple***

Dali's *Shirley Temple,* child-actress, child-virgin, is depicted not as Nabokov's Lolita, but as the Sphinx, as Kali, as dangerous to men especially in her innocence. This female child reigns over a death landscape of skulls, bones, a bat—a ship wrecked long ago. Here, we are not far from the increase in child prostitution and in child pornography magazines and movies—for commercial profit. Very *little* girls are already seductive and dangerous: because when they grow up they can reproduce the species. But all life dies: therefore, women can produce only corpses, women *are* the producers of death and therefore men must create religious ideologies that ensure or at least promise immortality and true life after death.

Mothers may weep goodbye or wave their sons into manhood with patriotic fervor, but they cannot prevent them from going. No need to. No matter how far a son may travel, he will never really leave home.

Never will man find a woman as able, as willing, to give birth to him again.

The son She saved is the son
she spoiled: by creating a furious
dependence on that which is forbidden—
Herself in other women. A son belongs
to his Mother forever, no matter how
many other women he leaves, no matter
how many other women he stays with.

Curious, subtle, tragic: this female
eunuch's revenge, this mother's truest
marriage.

Giovanni Bologna. ***The Neptune Fountain***

To me, this mermaid, this sexually explicit, ancient goddess-like figure is beautiful: commanding, powerful, sensual, sexual. Notice her place: as one of four women at the base of the Neptune statue.

Neptune, or Poseidon—and I personally was extremely moved by the temple to him at Sounion, in Greece—is, like most resplendent patriarchs, being held up by the labor of women, by women whose former power and current work remains unnoticed.

Bronzino. ***Allegory on Venus, Cupid, Time and Folly***

Bronzino's *Allegory* is the best painting I could find that depicts a truly erotic contact between a mother-figure (an "older" woman) and a son-figure (a "younger" boy or potential consort). Mother-son incest in real or surrogate forms occurs very rarely and is highly taboo. If fathers were once "replaced" by sons for erotic or reproductive purposes, then part of male-bonding or father-son truce would be based upon giving up the right to the Mother; this would also avoid rivalry and competition for her, and the presumed replaceability of older man by younger man. Under patriarchy, it would be women, not men, who would be "replaced" or interchangeable. In fact, father-daughter incest is the dominant psychosexual model between the sexes in modern society.

Bronzino's Venus and Cupid *are* lovely . . . and as Freud said: "A mother is only brought unlimited satisfaction by her relation to a son; that is altogether the most perfect, the most free from ambivalence of all human relationships."

4. PHALLIC SEXUALITY

DR.: *Have you ever wished you'd been born a girl?*
BOY: *Yes.*
DR.: *Why did you wish that?*
BOY: *Girls, they don't have to have a penis.*
DR.: *They don't have to have a penis?*
BOY: *They can have babies. . . .*
DR.: *Why do you think girls don't have to have a penis?*
BOY: *'Cause they have to have babies. . . . And babies can't come out of a penis . . . Babies come out of a vagina. . . .*
DR.: *Your penis gives you a nice feeling, doesn't it? You're not scared of it when it gets big and stiff, are you?*
BOY: *No.*
DR.: *Good! It's supposed to do that when you tickle it. That's one* big *advantage for being a boy, 'cause girls can't do that, you know.*
BOY: *Um hum.*
DR.: *Sure they can have babies, but only boys can have a penis stand up like that.*

Reported by Richard Green in *Sexual Identity Conflict in Children and Adults*

"I remember," she said, "how you pretended you did not know you were caressing a woman friend who was sitting on one side of you, while I sat on the other."

"What is wrong with that?"

"Nothing, except that later you insisted with great intensity that you had never done such a thing, that you never would do such a thing in my presence. But I think you did it, knowing you did not want to know, trying to hide it from yourself, pretending you were ignorant of what you did. You were like the Nazis, who pretended innocence and at the same time enjoyed the terror caused by their double game. You had played on my naïveté so many times, but this time I saw through you."

"Naïveté," observed the old man, "is not innocence. Perhaps true innocence would have defeated the devil of the double game."

"Yes, but I fell from innocence, after so many years of abused naïveté."

Hannah Tillich, writing about her husband, Paul Tillich, in *From Time to Time*

Man created God in the image of his own erect penis: a generative rock of ages, a staff of life, a divine obsession.

Buried female idols, tiny beneath the tent pegs, were unearthed, upended, beheaded, and, in full view, transformed into phalluses. Men marked their sacred crossings with them: pillars of fire, pillars of ash.

Unknown. "Female Idols": ***Breasts from Dolni Vestonice,*** **c.23,000 B.C.**

Men wanted this new God to be
the most powerful One, the only One.
Like children, they tested and
compared and measured His might, and His
size constantly: in miracles of
fertility, in miracles of battle.

Men's new God was jealous, demanding,
impatient—and couldn't be trusted.
There were times when men needed Him—
and He wasn't there. And there were times
when He wouldn't disappear—no matter
who else was watching. Like all Fathers.
Like all penises.

It was decided that no longer
could men spill God's sacred seed
on themselves or on their parents,
on their brothers, on their sisters,
or on their children. If men seeded
only their wives, their concubines,
their female slaves, and their prostitutes—
then their days and their
children would be numbered among
the stars.

Holy-ambitious, men copied God's
likeness on earth—lest they forget,
and because it was hard to overcome
the pagan habit of idol-making.

Men built great new cities filled
with endless reflections of God's motion,
God's language, God's action. Thundering
tools that bore down, that tunneled down
through earth to erect skyward structures
that tower unnaturally over people.
(Dictators live on the topmost floors.)
Phallic-shaped microphones that swell our
disembodied voices into Godly pronouncements.
Oil rigs, endlessly pumping away.

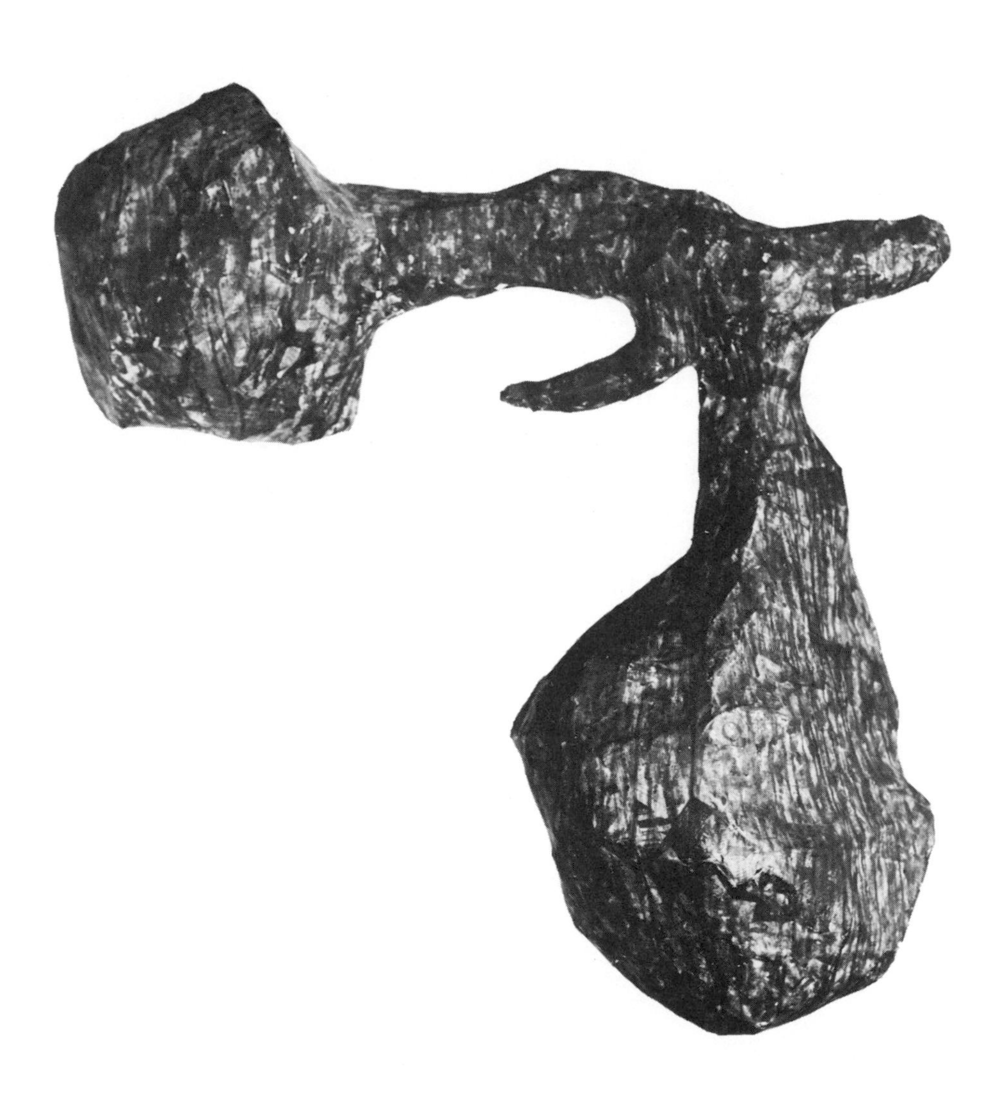

Claes Oldenburg. ***Empire (Papa) Ray Gun***

This is the description of Oldenburg's sculpture in a book devoted to his work: "A ray gun is a child's toy, but the *Empire (Papa) Ray Gun* is a magnificent phallic image. It is made of newspaper soaked in wheat paste, applied over chicken wire and painted with casein. The paper, yellowed with age, has taken on a dusty gold color which emerges through the grey-black paint and adds its tone to the aura of ancient mysteries which pervades the work. The Ray Gun image occurs again and again in Oldenburg's oeuvre; he identifies himself with it; it is a symbol of his manhood, his vision and his art."

Catholic childhood. Bodies rigid,
mouths silent, young boys learned to
celebrate the forbidden mass of
masturbation. The Church Fathers were merciless
in their punishment of all that tempted
them: women burned in the Inquisitor's
fires, beautiful Turkish infidels died
by the sword of Christian desire.

Protestant childhood. A manly rediscovery
of single driving forces: each
man armed with his own Rock of Enlightened
Principle. Now there was no stopping
the clean, sure blade of material history.
Apollo was already on His way to the moon.
The Protocols of the Elders of Auschwitz,
Hiroshima, and My Lai.

The industrial-sexual revolution.
The secular penis.
Having invested so much of its
seed in profitable machinery, it
is already sated, already spent.
Secular man need only push
buttons to be as powerful as God:
a self-sufficient phallic giant,
a triumphantly passive man-child.
The collective dream of countless
centuries of poor men. The Second
Eden.

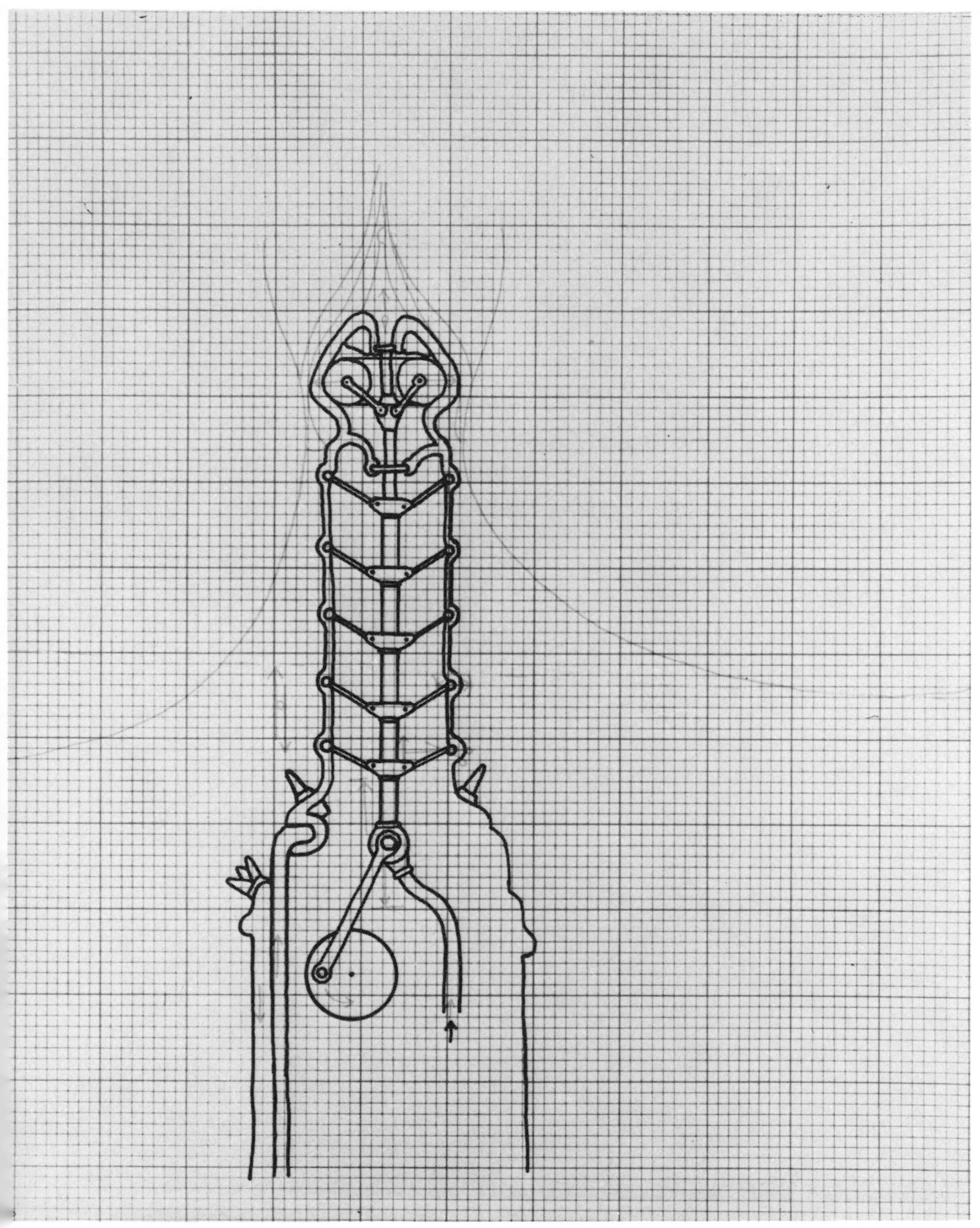

Tomi Ungerer. ***Untitled***

Ungerer's phallic-mechanical object is depicted on graph paper. Interestingly, the drawing is contained in a collection of "pornography" entitled *Fornicon*. Notice the tiny, sharp piercing "teeth" of the penile-drive-shaft device: they are meant to penetrate the softness of soft Earth, as well as the unyielding granite layers of earth that yield up to men oil, gold, coal, and other minerals.

The sacred penis. In Mecca, in Jidda,
in Rome, in Jerusalem, in Peking, in New York,
in ethnic enclaves everywhere, still, it is
Biblically active, still, men are enjoined
to marry, to multiply, and to plunder for God.

The sacred penis. Sons call on the
ancient God of their Fathers in order to
repossess the machines made of their own
flesh, in order to build their *own* machines
in the more ancient image of woman: yielding
profit annually, easily replaced,
subservient to man's will.

Sons or fathers, poor men or rich men, sacred or secular: all are homosexual in their worship of everything phallic. A sexual revolution might destroy what men do so well together, away from women: the making of His-story, the making of war, the triumph of phallic will.

Michelangelo. ***The Slave***

The "magnificent" Greek and Renaissance sculptures of nude men—hairlessly marble, frontally nude—have never aroused my sexual interest. I did not think that "high art" was supposed to, and when I looked at all those well-developed heroes, and athletes in tunics and loincloths, I *knew* that it was "great art" because I could stare at male penises—shaped as perfectly, as beautifully, as male musculature—without the slightest twinge of lust. This was well before I understood that "high art," as well as pornography, was meant to appeal to male and not to female "prurient" interest.

C. J. Bulliet, in *Venus Castina,* noted that "Greek sculptors immortalized the boys they loved, not only in the effeminate male figures of young athletes, Bacchuses, Ganymedes, Mercurys and Apollos, but in the slim, slender-hipped, small-breasted nymphs, Dianas, Graces, and Venuses."

Michelangelo, the one mighty genius of the Renaissance working in marble who could have broken the spell of the classic ideal, not only failed to do so, but helped fix the charm more securely. Michelangelo, even more certainly than Leonardo da Vinci, was a slave to male beauty . . . Nearly all Michelangelo's youthful male figures—with the exception, perhaps, of the gigantic David—deviate from the decidedly masculine and approach the mean, the human in the abstract; thus they seem to us imbued with a quality of femininity; they even exhibit decidedly female characteristics.

I have in mind first and foremost the youths depicted on the ceiling of the Sistine Chapel (the most soulful adolescent figures in the world), but also Bacchus, St. John, Adonis, and the figures in the background of the Holy Family at Florence. Cupid and David Apollo (in the Bargello) are almost hermaphroditic, and even the Adam, and the unfinished Slaves in the Boboli Gardens exhibit female characteristics. . . .

On the other hand—with the exception of two of his early Madonnas and, perhaps, Eve—he has not given us one glorified female figure; all his women are characterized by something careworn and unlovely; some of his old women—most strikingly the Cumaean Sybil—are depicted with absolute masculine features, masculine figures and gigantic musculature. . . .

Emil Lucka, quoted in C. J. Bulliet, *Venus Castina*

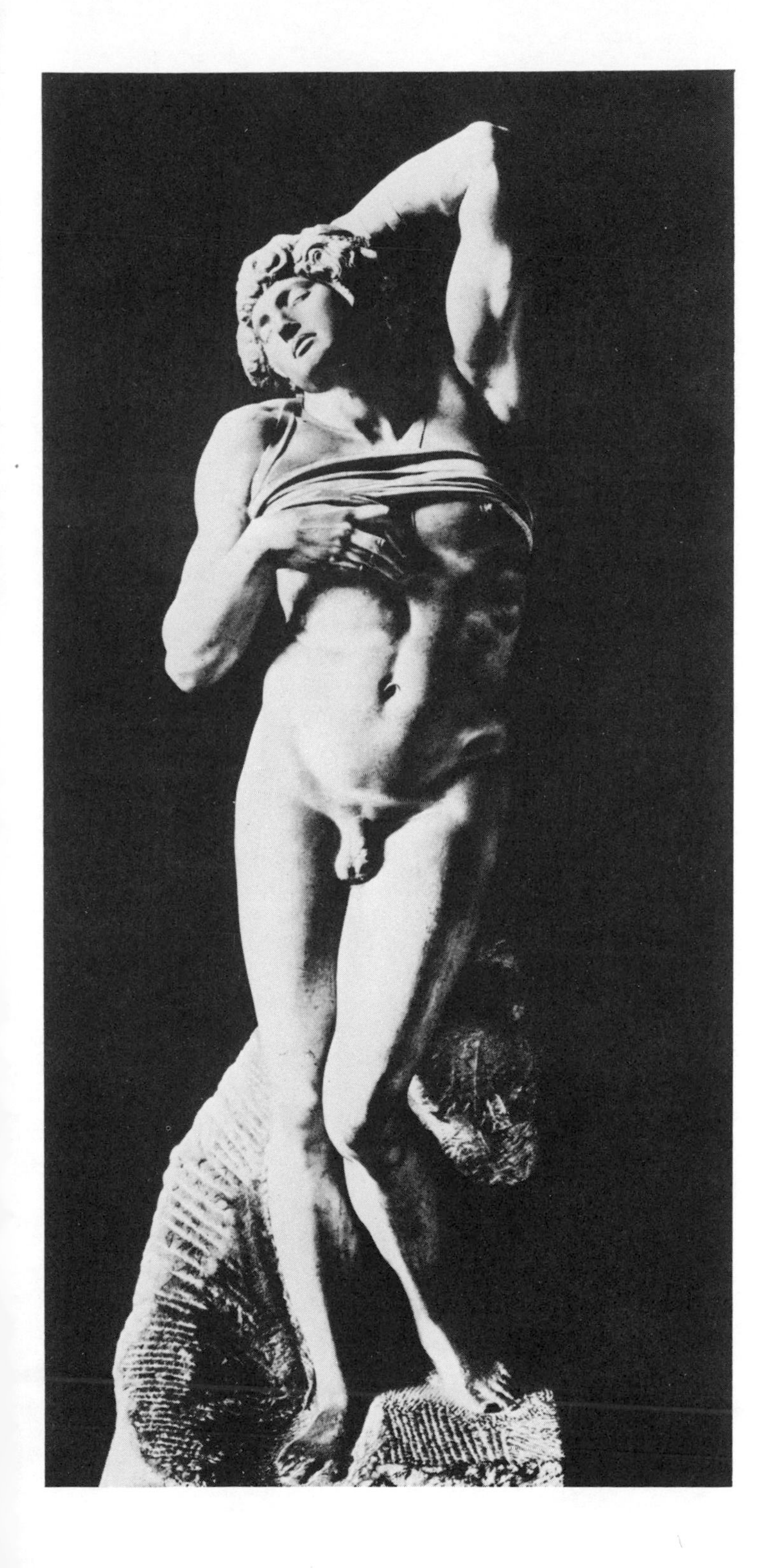

Sylvia Sleigh. ***Double Images: Paul Rosano***

I find this young man intensely and unashamedly beautiful. The canvas is life-sized and lushly colored. Sleigh has often had difficulty in exhibiting her male nudes. People—men and women—have demonstrated, brought pressure to bear, and upon occasion have had the "offending" frontally nude male canvases removed from public view.

In museums, everywhere, women are hanging, frontally nude. Couples, men of all ages, even middle-aged and elderly women, move arm in arm from one painting to the next, whatever fear, envy, spite, or sense of outrage they may have rendered totally silent by patriarchal conditioning. What, then, is the problem with viewing fully naked men today?

Perhaps men cannot bear the possibility of being compared secretly and endlessly—by *women*—to other men, to more youthful or to more beautiful men. Perhaps it is something else.

Sleigh, unlike da Vinci, Verrocchio, and Michelangelo, for example, paints her nude men for *women, as* a woman, and not necessarily for homosexual men, as a homosexual. She has broken with a very long tradition of narcissistic phallus worship, and of homosexual artistic adoration of male beauty. In her male nudes, she is not grafting certain feminine attributes onto youthful male models—lovers and apprentices—to create an Adam, a Christ, or a Virgin. Her male nudes, hairy, graceful, "virile" but not muscularly idealized, are not based on male narcissism, and therefore appeal to *women's* interest. This, I think, is the source of her "troubles," and the nature of her radicalism.

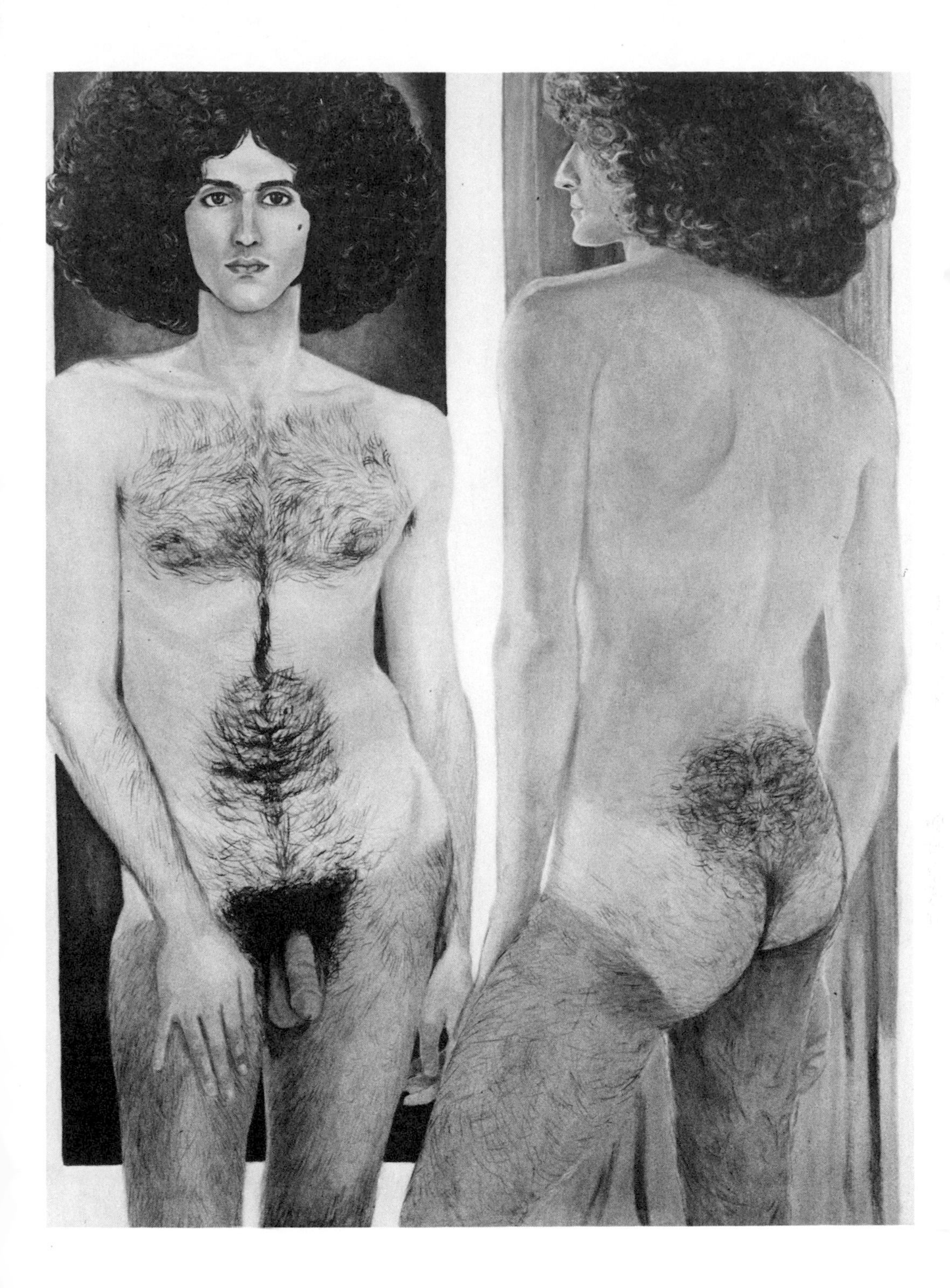

Henri Rousseau. *The Dream*.
1910. Oil on canvas, 6′8½″ x 9′9½″. Collection, The Museum of Modern Art,
New York. Gift of Nelson A. Rockefeller

Henri Rousseau. ***The Dream***

Not only are women painted or sculpted fully frontally naked, what is more fascinating is the degree to which women are fully naked in those very same paintings where men, bizarrely, are fully dressed, often in top hat, morning coats, cravat, monocle, etc. There are so many paintings of naked women on lawns, picnicking with men in formal attire that it would be entirely another project to show them to you here: those with or without the offending pubic or underarm hair, those at home, those sitting on balconies, those still ensconced in nature, being serenaded by lutes.

Henri Rousseau, in one of my favorite paintings, entitled *The Dream,* has a charming young woman (male painters do not often paint charming or beautiful old women) reclining on a Victorian couch, her frontally nude body facing us, surrounded by a wondrous collection of friendly plants and animals. There is a black man in the painting too, playing a musical instrument, but his penis is hidden by a many-colored loincloth. Even in a dream, a fantasy of Eden, we are not allowed to see the sacred male penis; even here, in full comic innocence, even in *nature,* the male penis is too sacred, or too vulnerable, to be displayed.

"He asked me if I had ever made love with my father. I looked at him and kind of giggled and I said, 'No.' And he said, 'Have you ever thought about making love with your father?' I said 'Yes.' And he told me, 'All right, when you are making love . . . picture in your mind that I am your father.' And I did. I did so, and it was a very beautiful experience."

Susan Atkins, aka Sadie Mae Glutz, a "Manson Girl," under legal examination. From Vincent Bugliosi and Curt Gentry, *Helter Skelter*.

Albrecht Altdorfer. ***Lot and His Daughter***

Altdorfer has captured the "depraved," lecherous, or animalistic face of father-daughter incest. Here we again see a male parent alone with his children: the female parent is missing or presumed dead, either in childbirth, in divorce, or due to female evil or foolishness. In this case, Lot's wife "looked back"—and was turned into a pillar of salt. Looking back was an act of compassion and mourning, and yet her punishment was instant. I have never heard her human gesture and its punishment mourned by scholars or nonscholars, as, by contrast, the longing of Orpheus has been.

The dominant model of Relationship between the sexes in patriarchal culture is that of father-daughter incest. Young virgin daughter-figures are meant to mate with and/or marry experienced father-figures for whom they will produce divine male offspring. There are several psychological interpretations of Lot's particular story. One is the female child's repressed and not so repressed wish to replace her mother—to flee her mother—and find freedom in sleeping with her father. Another interpretation or justification for father-daughter incest is in terms of species survival: given mother and infant mortality rates traditionally, men must have ever-younger womb-men available to them for reproductive purposes.

A third interpretation of the Lot story is a more unusual one.

Mary Cahn Schwartz in *Lilith* magazine (1976–1977) notes that "Lot's daughters, . . . after Sodom and Gomorrah have been destroyed, fear they are left alone on earth, with only an ineffectual father. The two sisters plan together how they will people their world. With remarkable sibling harmony, rarely seen in 'Genesis', they plan together. They get their father drunk; each then takes her turn lying with him; each gets pregnant, and each satisfies her mission. What is different about these women from the rest of the females in 'Genesis' is that they are totally isolated from their society; they are setting up whatever brave new world they can construct and they are not bound by any traditional female role."

Jean-Auguste-Dominique Ingres. ***Jupiter and Thetis***

This painting shows us a supreme male deity: remote, majestic, symmetrical, immovable—very much in contrast to the fluid profile of the female half-deity, Thetis. Here we see male frontality, but in full majestic covering. We do not see Jupiter's penis frontally. Thetis, a nymph, a vulnerable daughter-figure, is beseeching Jupiter to avenge an insult to her son, Achilles.

It seems to me that even if the supple, swan-necked supplicant brings Jupiter to orgasm orally as he sits on the throne, Jupiter's patriarchal position would have him betray as little emotion as possible, as little loss of control as possible—even if he is receiving sexual pleasure. Certainly, Jupiter is unmoved by the troubled, watchful jealousy of his wife in the left-hand corner. . . .

How forgetful, how ungrateful, the sons of mothers are: after all, Jupiter himself was saved by his mother from being devoured by his father Saturn!

How grotesquely faithful mother-reared or mother-saved sons are: they treat all other women as secondary. Jupiter, like so many mother-protected sons, is not fluid or emotional in his eroticism, is not sexually monogamous, is not used to displays of heterosexual *giving,* vulnerability, or emotion.

Peellaert. ***The Rolling Stones***

5. BROTHERS

Albrecht Dürer. ***Cain Killing Abel***

This woodcut depicts the primal, brutal way in which most men act out brotherhood. Despite "old boys' clubs"; despite father-son reconciliations; despite a verbal call for "brotherhood"; despite Judaism, Christianity, Islam, Hinduism, Buddhism, Communism, Existentialism, Humanism, most ideologies, when translated into human, mortal practice, do not lead to the love of blood-brother for blood-brother, nor to the love of "brother" for "brother."

"When you go to women," says Nietzsche, "take your whip with you." Sensible despots have never confined that precaution to women: they have taken their whips with them when they have dealt with men, and been slavishly idealized by the men over whom they have flourished the whip much more than by women.

Bernard Shaw, *Pygmalion*

Blood-brothers: men who
share the same womb. Blood-brothers:
men who share the same paternal sperm.
Blood-brothers: warriors who share
another man's blood.

Murder offers unlimited
possibilities of brotherhood. After
all, how many brothers can one womb
produce?

Once, fratricide threatened
the Houses of Man: as soon as fathers
allowed all their sons to live. This
fratricidal impulse had to be turned
outward, away from Home. This
family feeling had to be expressed
some other way: in tribal warfare,
in religious warfare, in nation warfare,
in nuclear warfare.

The Houses of Men are founded
upon such sublimations.

After he makes the touchdown,
he magic-slaps each teammate's palms
and they his ass: fraternal reassurances
of *communal* victory, ritual reminders
of what must be avoided. Reminded,
the warriors turn their brotherly
rage outward, toward the men in foreign
uniforms. Laws, commandments—the
handshakes mysterious to women. The
harmless sport of fratricide.

Francisco Goya. ***Wonderful Heroism! Against Dead Men!***

The mutilation after death of men by men is a common wartime practice. It maddened Goya—but even he, the master of gruesome detail, could not bring himself to reveal graphically the sexual castration of men by men. Certainly, it is implied, but the missing genitalia are nowhere to be seen. The severed head retains unbearable Spanish dignity: mute, proud, eyes closed to the landscape of male savagery.

Francisco Goya. *The Third of May, 1808, in Madrid*

Grown men, Fathers, wearing the
uniforms of their youth, are marching
today on Fifth Avenue, in favor of war.
It is a march of the ugly schoolchildren,
bearing the beer bellies, the bad teeth,
the oily foreheads of the industrial poor—
protesting the Health, the Beauty, the Grace
of which they were cheated. The men grin in
place, shuffle sheepishly, still waiting to
be told what to do. They are too old to fight.
But their sons are the right age.

How homo-social: the sadistic snap of
a hand salute, the slow-moving ass of a policeman's
horse. Rifles and drum rolls: this is
male bacchanal. Male war-ecstasy. The Brotherhood
of Death. This is the love permitted
between fathers and sons, and between brothers.

Only such unrequited love between
family men could fill each century's quota
for corpses, each grinning century's quota
for warriors.

Warriors: the virile feminine: a
shower of classical coins, golden male
profiles, equestrian statues, powerful martial
joy. Patroclus and Achilles, Jonathan and
David. Love among brothers.

Peter Paul Rubens. ***Allegory of War***
Jacques-Louis David. ***Battle of the Romans and Sabines***

In Rubens' *Allegory of War* and David's *Battle of the Romans and Sabines,* we see women attempting to stop men, with their own unarmed bodies, from killing *other men and children.* They do not appear to succeed. This is because of the public powerlessness of mothers and the absence of "maternal" virtues from military and political activities. Most mothers have no power to stop this "senseless male killing" of the children, their own and the children of other mothers. No military force in the world requires a permission note from mothers before sons—or daughters—are drafted into war.

But men tell me that war
is hell, and that heroic Warriors,
heroic brothers, no longer exist.
I believe them. For example,
Heroes have always needed to leave
home for at least twenty years.
Where could a Hero go today that
is *not* home? There are Pepsi-
Cola signs in every desert, every
valley, every city of the world,
dollar signs in the hearts of all
men. Now, we are one Tribe, at
war with itself.

It is no longer
Heroic to fly over fiery mountains on winged
horses: all air passengers do. Only the men
in lunatic asylums take a real flight, only
those who see it at the bottom of the well of
their brown paper wine bottles.

Only madmen think they're Christ—
and as many think they're Napoleon. All men
have blueprints for Final Solutions, even the
men who are made to sit in their own shit.

Men in corporate elevators,
standing still, rising up, each
dressed in regulation suit, hat,
expression. What if I want to speak
to this man here? What if I can't?
What if he's not been programmed to
respond and goes berserk, goes to pieces?
The other men stare straight ahead, waiting
to get off.

René Magritte. ***The Son of Man***

The son of man, Man's son: faceless, anonymous, well-suited for 1984. This son's identity, his face, remains ever-longingly obliterated by the events of Eden, by the temptation of the Apple.

Protected, numbed, numbered, by money, machines, and modernity, man is still fixed upon the themes I have written about in "Male Images: Reflections of Eden": his relationship to his devouring male and female parents; his fear, longing, and confusion over blood: the blood of circumcision, of crucifixion, and of childbirth.

Man's son still feels damned and exiled. Still, he desires, longs for, *demands,* and moves heaven and earth in order to get redeemed, in order to be assured of immortality and innocence.

Lately, our scientists have
reported strange sightings on their
radar screens: black and yellow giants,
packs of masked and screaming women—
and what seems to be a plague of bugs.
Bugs in the spaces behind their eyes,
bugs that penetrate from behind and
erupt from within, a bug in the System,
aliens in our midst. The return of
the oppressed.

The industrial male poor: buckle beatings, factory whistles, a childhood of imprisoned Sundays—that Cemetery Day when you worship the Dead Son, visit the dead grandparents, eat together in dead silence. Which of these men wants to be a Lover or a Saint? The child you laugh at, feel sorry for, don't play with—until it's time to crucify him.

Most men would rather be members of the mob on Golgotha—and not the guy alone on the cross. And so it has gone, among brothers.

What troubled the young mother most of all was the eyes, one dark and one light green, as though belonging to two different persons.

The old saltwater blacks, rich in experience, told her that this was what happened when the mixture of bloods takes place too quickly and without pleasure: in ditches, by the roadside, and especially on slave ships. For on a specified day, a month before the ship was due to reach port, the black women were washed in sea water and the drunken sailors allowed to make free with them. The children of the "pariade", as this strange custom was called, often had conflicting features . . . And that was the case with this poor seedling . . . conceived on shipboard in the frenzy and confusion.

Bayangumay despaired as she had done during her pregnancy, when night after night in her dreams she had seen a little white man with a whip in his hand coming out of her womb.

At the chevalier's bidding, her body was drenched in musk and ointments, creams and perfumes. She was fitted out with bracelets and anklets, with Creole necklaces and strings of gold and silver ornaments, with coral and garnet earrings. This costume, known at the time as "la pimpante", was topped off by a bright yellow madras which gave her the absent exotic look of a parrot. The chevalier was moved by her air of strange melancholy.

She began to scream at night . . . In her nightmare, always the same, she saw herself changed into a sugar statue, which the Frenchmen of France were slowly eating far, far away at the other end of the world, first breaking off her fingers, so thin and long that they seemed unreal.

André Schwarz-Bart, *A Woman Named Solitude*

Paul Cadmus. *To the Lynching!*
1935. Pencil and watercolor on paper, 20½"x 15¾". Collection of Whitney Museum of American Art

Paul Cadmus. ***To the Lynching!***

The political and spiritual dismemberment of dark men: the capture, the sale, the betrayal of dark-skinned men by other dark-skinned men—to white-skinned men, who bore their African captives into slavery in Catholic Europe, in Catholic-European South America, in Moslem Asia, in the Protestant United States. The madness of slavery captured in one explosive image: the lynching, the torture, the castration, the hanging of black men by white men; the "strange fruit" on Southern trees.

Cadmus' swirls of violence show us how hard it is for men to act gently, lovingly, with a sure sense that every fellow creature is "brother" and not "stranger."

Who wants to be a Hero or a Warrior?
How many men dare denounce the many killers
for hire—the many vain and dreadful men,
the many bankers and surprisingly short
colonels who rule by torture and deceit?
The many politicians who only follow orders,
who have families to feed? . . .

Our planet's rulers: how few understand
the meaning or the consequences of their actions.
But do not underestimate them: they hold the
mortgage to our lives.

Fernando Botero. *The Presidential Family*. 1967.
Oil on canvas, 80⅛″ x 77¼″. Collection, The Museum of Modern Art, New
York. Gift of Mr. Warren D. Benedek

Fernando Botero. ***The Presidential Family***

This grotesque-comic portrait of a Family in Power constitutes an acid portrait of the patriarchal family and nation-state. The family members, even their pet dog, are look-alikes: squat, bloated, infantile, vain—stereotypes, not human beings.

Most of us dream the long dream of sentiment and romance. We dream of Vermeer's domestic yellows, of family harmony, stability, security, and love. Most of us are unwilling, even unable, to see any resemblance between the impossibly human romantic illusion etched on our hearts and the reality mirrored for us in Botero's painting.

Mauricio Lasansky. ***The Nazi Drawings***

Lasansky is a survivor who in his drawings is still there, in the Nazi camps, so that we view his work as a continuing rehearsal of the drama of what it means to have survived that experience.

In the crudely blood-bedaubed collage of the eighteenth drawing, the cruciform motif takes precedence, leaping to the eye with a force that is hard to account for. Not only is the central maternal figure clearly shown being impaled by the newsprint cross, but there is also an arm, either her own or a disembodied one, visible below her terrible head and pulling the string that is hoisting the popeyed figure up on the cross. At the same time, as if unaware of the horror, the infant lies on its mother's belly—asleep or dead, it is hard to tell which. In another refinement of motif, the crossbar is here made into a newspaper collage with a clipping in it about an actual SS killer named Kaduk.

With [Lasansky's] twentieth drawing a new kind of motif proliferation occurs—the concentration camp numbers, repeated in drawing after drawing.

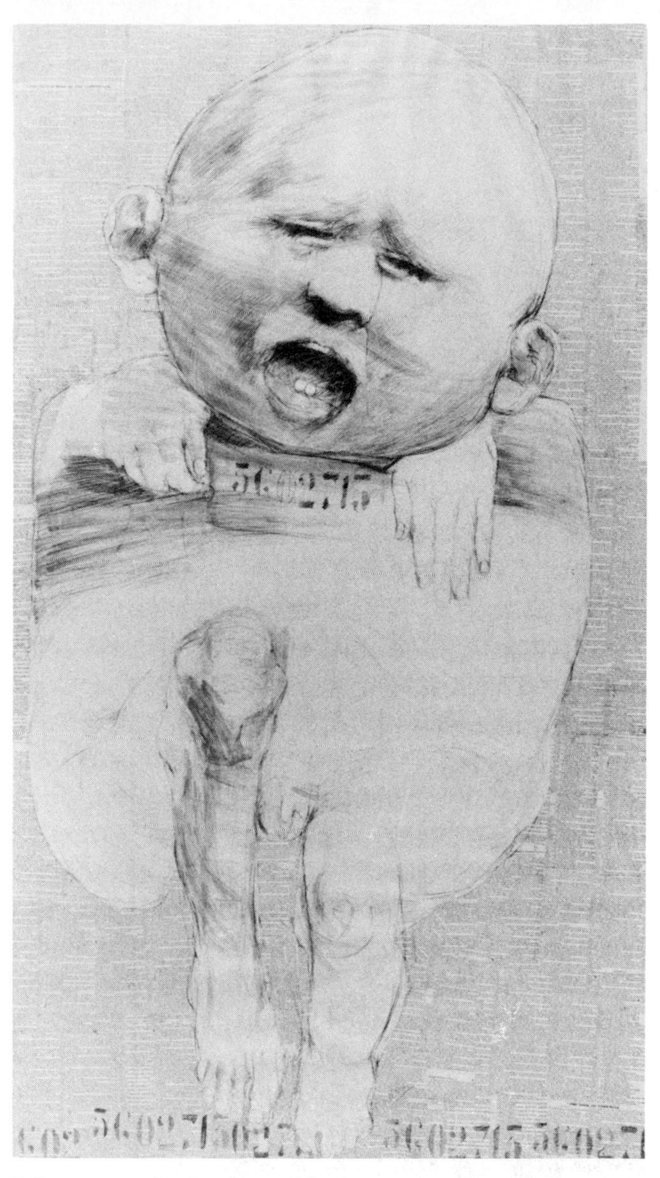

A final series of five portraits begins with the twenty-fourth drawing, and these are the counterparts to the solemnly murderous, skull-helmeted, encased killer figures introduced in the first four drawings. Here the victim children are caught in the midst of their terrible grief and final suffering, with swollen heads enlarged against their small, useless, disproportionate hands, as if they themselves had become the personifications of the nightmare they are being subjected to. The tireless repetition of the same tattooed concentration camp number seems to perforate each of these drawings except the twenty-fifth, which bears no number at all, perhaps because it is the embodiment of a wordless scream. Collages, pencilled webs, retracted lips over horror-grinning teeth . . . the reiterated motifs come together in a crescendo of simple, unanswerable deprivation.

From the Introduction by Edwin Honig to Mauricio Lasansky, *The Nazi Drawings*

For a man to "understand" too much,
or to ask too many "questions," leads to slow
and painful castration by other men—and men
would rather settle the matter quickly.

Last year, a young man told me that
he felt uncontrollably vulnerable whenever he
experienced empathy for the suffering of others.
"It tears me apart. I feel castrated," he said.
"I'd rather have a group of guys coming at me
with knives than feel this awful feeling."

Bea Kreloff. *Untitled*

There is something infantile, and something powerless, in Kreloff's grown man, drowning: Is he wearing baby booties—or astronaut boots? Is he on display in some horrible human experiment—or is he on TV, a hero in action?

Bea Kreloff has painted many men in institutions: hulking, sightless, mutely resigned to a prisoner's fate; great, silent reminders of our social guilt and shame. Her portraits of men speak to me of the countless burned-out male casualties, the male body-count involved in male heroics; the spiritual bankruptcy of Father-rule and Father-worship—or as Gabriel Marquez has named it, The Autumn of the Patriarch.

Yes, and now I wish to praise men
who have loved their brothers. Men
who have protected each other—not
only from women, but from other,
more powerful men. Men who have
"understood" too much. But my mouth
is dry with fear and boredom: they
have fathered their own martyrdom
so often, they have fathered my
undoing always, they have killed so
many other men in the name of
brotherly love—and I have done with
the worship of Death.

Käthe Kollwitz. ***The Parents***

. . . how useless everything we do becomes
when faced with color photos of the atrocities.

One baby in the heap squirmed to find the wet breast
of its dead mother, habit having had just time enough
to teach: Breast equals Safety
—though how explain this red milk? Next
the child, too, was shot,
then finished off with the stab of a bayonet,
carved into three neat pieces
before being thrown away. Not any words,
not any any any words I can teach you,
my precious baby, can say back the cries
strangled in your stabbed throat,
no introduction to any analysis
equal to explaining what has happened to a country
that pays $40,000 for color photos
of the atrocities but will not buy
enough milk to keep its own babies from starving.

Stop. All of it. Stop taking courses
like this one. Wipe them out of the catalog.
Replace them with Introduction to
Malnutrition; Intermediate Butchery; Advanced
Ecological Suicide.

Kenneth Pitchford, *Color Photos of the Atrocities*

PART TWO

MALE REALITIES: AUTOBIOGRAPHICAL PORTRAITS

The First Man: My Father

My First Husband: Men in Iranistan

Men at School

Men in New York City

Men at Work

Men at Home

1. THE FIRST MAN: MY FATHER

Summer, 1943. My earliest memory: my father naked in the shower, singing to me in Yiddish, his penis white, oh so white, and rising, like the steam, like my pleasure, like my mother's shocked voice: "Close the curtains, get her out of there." I was three years old.

My paternal grandmother's house: a long dark hallway to Sunday's parlor, the sun prim over the sofa doilies, the wrapped candies, the glassed-in Talmuds. Dark skirts of women moving, serving, at their genetic ease.

Her stepson, my father: orphaned in Poland at eight, his mother killed before his eyes, and then again at twelve, his father dying in America. He had to quit school when he was twelve. He drove taxis and long-distance trailers, rode horses, cooked in short-order diners and luncheonettes—all before I met him. When I knew him, he drove his own truck, up and down Brooklyn streets, selling soda, seltzer, beer and day-time conversation.

I loved to sit next to him on the truck. I came to love the smell of gasoline, male sweat, and garages; came to love all the boys who wore short leather jackets and huge silver crosses and were as silent as adults when an adult came into their midst. My mother knew them for what they were: gas station attendants, construction workers, poolroom bums. But I and my father were kin to them.

My father: the first man I ever knew. The first man I ever loved. The first man who wouldn't marry me. (Can it really be that I have never swayed over a knife with my mother's blood on it? No, I have loved her too darkly and truly.)

But I would have run away with her husband. Why didn't he wake me before he left for work at 6:00 A.M., whispering, "Be quiet" and "I've packed your dress, your books, your eyeglasses, and rubber bands for your braids. We're going. Shhh. Don't wake your mother. She's tired."

Daddy: with what difficulty you braided my long hair. How quickly you slapped me if I moved around too much. How ill-at-ease you felt doing this "woman's work"; how lovingly you did it.

Even as a child, I knew that nothing but their children occupied my parents, united them, divided them. Their reign as adults extended only as long as their first child's dependence. At four, I crept along the walls of their tyranny, fresh with fear, already pinched with migraines, wearing clear plastic glasses that were nearly as large as my face. At night, I always held my breath in bed, imagined I was Cinderella—and then had nightmares of haunted houses and my own death.

From the beginning, my mother understood that things would not "turn out all right." Somehow, her nine-year-old daughter had already given up her place in line for a boy genius in boxer trunks on the side of his own swimming pool. It was clear to her that I would someday live in a furnished room, and take drugs, and wear gypsy rags, and be irretrievably haunted at thirty. And she had no means of quieting me: no cashmere sweaters, no trips to Florida. Her husband, my father, worked hard and had no money.

Summers, he sent us with shopping bags and extra sweaters and mealtime arguments to the half-full, barnlike hotels in the Catskill Mountains, with the flowered oilcloth on the tables and the showers down the hall smelling of must and failure and an early bedtime.

No one all summer ever had my father's tales of Cossack or landlord terror, of flight and disillusionment to tell me. The other guests, in new cotton clothing, "belonged" only to their own often imagined funerals. They held themselves aloof from one another, the memoryless but faithful descendants of a hundred villages, each of whose chief rabbis were feuding. Or were they already city people, riding an elevator together, suspicious and cheated? When the card games and the naps were over, the sun set palely over the ramshackle buildings, saving its magical purples and reds for the other hotels, where women in skimpy, sequined dresses could be heard laughing helplessly, late at night.

What does my father do all during the week without me, away from me?

When the schoolyard gossip finally reached my mother's ears, she confided in my father. He rushed upstairs, my mother yelling after him not to leave the truck unlocked, unwatched.

I am having milk and cookies with some girlfriends. "A tramp! That's what I sweat my guts out for. This is what I have to come home to."

I don't stop eating my cookie. I look at my father, chewing slowly. (I know how much *he* likes me sitting on his lap.) He lunges across the table at me.

"Not on the face," my mother screams. My parents reach me together, my mother hanging on to her husband's arm, while he fumbles his belt out of his pants. Their cheeks are flushed.

"Keep outta my way," he warns his wife. "You're gonna cry," he pants. "I'll give you something to cry about!" I begin screaming.

He drags me over his lap and pulls down my bloomers. My ass brings growls to his throat. He crashes down on my flesh, first with the strap, then with his hands. My mother weighs his arm down with each blow. My girlfriends shrink together, horrified and curious. My younger brother watches from the doorway, giggling, glad it isn't him.

"Shut up or you'll get it next," my father yells at him. Soon, both my younger brothers will know less father-love and even more father-violence than I. Soon, they will turn against each other and toward my mother for protection—in ways unimaginable and closed to me.

"I'm not a bum, goddamn it. I don't drink, I don't run around. I bring all my money home. What do you want from me? Your mother would never in a million years do what you do. Where did you learn this from? What's itching you? You don't get enough to eat? Your bed isn't soft enough? Do we close the house to your friends? Why do you break my heart?"

(Daddy, Daddy, not this way. I am named after your mother and I am not dead. Do not kill me.)

He begins to cry. His voice grows hoarse. He drops the strap on the floor. "Nothing comes easy, nothing. What I wouldn't have done to have a mother, a father, take care of me."

He sits on a kitchen chair for a while and then begins stumbling around the room, not knowing what he's doing home at this lunchtime hour.

At midnight, death slaps me awake and leads me to the silent image of my father's coffined profile. Sometimes, now, he comes in through the window to visit, wearing his floppy, apologetic hat and the tweed "suburban" coat my mother picked out for him. He smells of the steam from that shower he took during my third summer, when I watched him, beautifully naked, singing a Yiddish song. He dies of a heart attack shoveling winter snow when I am twenty-six.

I inherit no family heirlooms: no candlesticks, no pierced gold earrings, no inscribed Bible hastily smuggled out before they burn the ghetto down once more. I inherit his soft, large lips, and my own future.

2. MY FIRST HUSBAND: MEN IN IRANISTAN

Summer, Jahbad, Iranistan, 1961. The bazaar: a cacophony of hanging hammered silver, Swiss watches, yard goods, and sheep carcasses. Loud Indian music, the Jahbad River, the Himalayan foothills—all running through, ringing round, the exquisite egg-shell blue mosque, the tea shop, the ten-year-old boy bearing tea to the men in the government office. A caravan of camels passes by. Always, sheeted in black, from head to foot, there are women: silent, moving islands in a sea of men.

Child-beggars roam the streets, wearing the cosmetics of trachoma and parasitic infestations. I've seen them before, in Teheran, in Kabul, in Beirut. Now, in Jahbad, their mothers wait for them again, behind buildings and narrowed into doorways. The children pluck at my coat buttons, my purse, my packages, they scream after my retreating figure until they sight a new quarry. One child waves his crutches, another his withered arm stumps in the air: makeshift sideshows of horror. Some passersby laugh at them, call them tricksters, devils, rich people in disguise. Only a fool—or a foreigner—would give them any money.

There is something haunting, something familiar, in the muezzin's call, something known to me about the crowds that tumble out into the mosque's outer courtyard.

Bare foot to bare foot, equals under the dome, equals under the sun, equals, for the moment, before Allah. The men kneel toward Mecca to pray. This single, mass movement is surprisingly aggressive, surprisingly graceful. Their collective prostrate form provides a curious, almost political immunity. Gossips, or assassins, would hesitate before such an open protestation of faith.

Unknowingly, I have wandered into our human past. It is a relief, finally, to enter the archetype of the Family of Man, in a slightly tarnished, but still unbroken form. Here I can sit down in the lap of the Tribe, with my ancestors still whole, and quite visible.

What is dangerously submerged, and even more dangerously denied in Western minds, walks unself-consciously about in Iranistan: existing, prevailing, taken for granted.

In Iranistan, I first became sensitive to the deadly and complicated love-play among men. Here, where the center still holds, I was able to see how normally powerful, how normally cruel, fathers are to sons; and how daily, how familial an occurrence fratricide is.

Here, in a "foreign" place, I learned to see what was hidden in more familiar Western places. Here, where male rivalry seemed to resolve itself in a highly ritualized separation of the sexes, I began to understand that men, not women, are the deadliest killers of men on earth.

A PATRIARCH

Abdul Mohammed, or Agha Jaan (Dear Master), is in his sixties. I am twenty, the foreign bride of his third-born son, gone from him for ten years, to study in America, and now returned with me. My father-in-law, six feet from his black velvet eyes to his black Italian shoes, comes forward to greet me at the Jahbad airport. He stands his six feet gracefully, lithely, carefully. His black hair is thick and only flecked with gray at the temples; he has a broad, frank mustache; his eyes, before he puts his dark glasses back on, are seductive, commanding, silent.

Agha Jaan has dutifully exhausted two wives and is now, almost politely, exhausting his third and youngest wife, a woman in her late thirties. He has twenty-four children and four grandchildren. A devout Moslem, he never drinks alcohol or smokes, and doesn't permit his sons to do so in his presence. His children always greet him by executing a quick, cringing half-bow, as they simultaneously snatch his hand to kiss it.

He eats alone, in a sitting room hushed by thick maroon carpets and velvet drapes. Maryam, his fourteen-year-old daughter by his third wife, serves him each dish, bowing in and out of the room, like a servant.

After dinner, Abdul Mohammed walks through the garden alone. He doesn't like his children or his wives to disturb him with requests for favors or advice. His family understood nothing.

Once, long ago, Abdul Mohammed sat in jail awaiting execution. He had been a friend of the king who unveiled the women, who built hospitals, schools, and trolley cars. The king who remembered to take a tiny jar of Irani earth with him when he fled into exile.

Abdul Mohammed escaped also, into India. After five years, he was allowed to return.

Now, my father-in-law is as guarded, as philosophical, as diplomatic with his memories as he is with the ministers, the mullahs, the businessmen, and the foreigners who come for tea.

Once, when I lay dying of hepatitis, Abdul Mohammed came to pray in my room. When no one else was there, he spoon-fed me custard, and sadly, but craftily, told me that his sons were not really "men." "I am still taller than any of my sons."

SONS AND BROTHERS

Abdul Mohammed was his sons' favorite topic of conversation. His activities—and person—entranced them. They spent hours trying to outguess his next "maneuver": it was the only control they had over it. *They* were their father's real wives. Despite their bouts of melancholy, self-pity, and bitterness, they still flushed with pleasure when their father openly favored or complimented any one of them. Even fraternal rivalry was dispelled in their discussions of anything their father promised, did, or said. Their lives were totally in his hands.

Hamid is about thirty-three years old. He is the eldest son of Zamarut, the first wife. Ali and Ibrahim, my husband, are Zamarut's second- and third-born sons. Ali is thirty and Ibrahim is twenty-eight. Rashid is the eldest son of Rozia, the second wife. He is exactly Ali's age—thirty—but has far less status than any of Zamarut's sons.

All three brothers, Hamid, Rashid, and Ali work for their father in positions analogous to their order of birth. Their salaries are token. They make no decisions. Everything belongs to Abdul Mohammed. They are still the "boys."

Actually, Ali is his father's chauffeur, tea pourer, and messenger-intermediary. He carries over the letters for his father's signature, in a tentative, heavy-footed gait, hands fluttering from apology to supplication. Ali's carefully worked out plans for expansion are only glared at under thin paternal spectacles, and then dismissed.

"*Boroo, boroo* [go away]," his father tells him, "Go visit your future in-laws."

Ali, plans in hand, goes to sit, vacant-eyed, in front of the Russian potbellied stove, sipping tea, and keeping an erect back for the two overworked and underpaid clerks who sit behind him.

Ibrahim, my husband, has just returned from ten much-envied years abroad. Hamid and Ali treat their brother politely, but warily. They don't know yet what their intentions toward him should be: Ibrahim may be "raised above himself" by Abdul Mohammed or by the King. If he is not forced to assume his "natural" place under his father's control, in the family business, as the third son, then they would have to "watch out" for him, have to turn his advantage into their own—somehow.

For his and their own good, Ibrahim would have to be purged of his foreign and dangerous "idealism." The Western-educated brother must be quickly and sharply reminded to fear the gossip of frightened men—fear it far more than the disdain or disappointment of brave men. "Hotheadedness" and "impatience" must be "cooled off." Most returning Irani university graduates are given minor, poorly paid government positions in areas totally unrelated to their specialty, and then carefully watched: by suspicious fathers and brothers, by uneducated superiors, by jealous competitors.

Ibrahim felt some kinship for Ali. Ali had spent five years in Paris, Ibrahim, ten in New York. Like most Irani students, their allowance was strictly regulated by the government and was never enough to live on—not without some discomfort, not without some humiliation. Yet the money they *did* receive every month was more than they could have earned in Jahbad in a year. And their father had refused "on principle" to supplement their allowances, regardless of their host country's impossibly high standards of living.

When Ali's schooling was over, his allowance had been immediately withdrawn. His government summoned him home. Abdul Mohammed picked a bride out for him. After five years away, Ali was ready to claim what belonged to him. He would live a more comfortable life in Iranistan than he could, on his own, in Europe. Maybe through the foreign service he could return to Europe.

The government didn't need a college graduate in engineering. They needed a junior file clerk in the Ministry of Mines. Ali took to his room—"to think things over." He stayed there for nearly a year. When he emerged, he agreed to the marriage and went to work for his father.

Abdul Mohammed was building Ali and his fiancée their own new house. Moreover, Ali was allowed to spend hours *talking* with his fiancée. . . .

Hamid, the eldest son, was deeply jealous. Hamid lived with his wife, his children, his mother, and his younger, unmarried brothers in the large house he'd grown up in. And Hamid had met *his* wife for the first time at their wedding. Which was as it should be. Yet, wasn't he, Hamid, as smart, as modern, and basically *more* important than his younger, foreign-educated brother? Hamid's resentment wasn't tempered by the fact that Ali had as little control over his "new" house as Hamid had in occupying an "old" one.

Each night, Ibrahim appeared in a cloud of younger brothers, buoyant with gossip. Jahbad hadn't changed: Jahbad had changed *completely.* Tor and Naim, Zamarut's college-age sons, *both* looked like Abdul Mohammed.

Tor and Naim addressed me in English, carefully, emphatically, as "sister-in-law." They were the family clowns who improvised, cleverly, on Irani society. They impersonated Iranis so caught up in greeting each other, or in gossip, that they missed appointments, or were killed by enemy fire. They played bureaucrats swollen with importance and misinformation, marriage brokers, mullahs, town idiots, shopkeepers.

"Sister-in-law, listen about my teacher," Naim reminisced. The teacher, a mullah, had installed himself in a comfortable room, demanded and received a servant and a huge supply of tobacco and sweets. Then he proceeded to teach young Naim the alphabet. Every day, for two weeks, he taught and retaught him the first letter of the Persian alphabet—*alif.*

"But, sister-in-law," Naim told me, "I was reading ahead secretly all the time. Then, when mullah asks me again, again,

again, to tell him '*alif,*' I jump up, I yell, 'Mullah, *bey, bey,* I know *bey.*' " (Of course, Naim had to apologize and finish out his lessons at the mullah's pace. But so what?, Naim's eyes pleaded. For once, the Emperor's nakedness had been challenged.)

An American diplomat put it this way: "We can't impose our 'moral' or 'cultural' values on these people. We can't ask them about their system of government or justice, their treatment of women, their servants, their jails. These are very sensitive, very touchy, very proud men—who happen to own a piece of land that's important to us. If we aren't careful, their kids would be learning Russian—or Chinese—instead of English and German. You've got to remember, we're guests here, not conquerors."

Yes. Diplomats have no responsibility for Irani schoolchildren, beautiful with promise and spontaneity—before they are crushed, muted, shamed, and bored into hopelessness by rigid, fearful, and poorly educated teachers. Americans—and Russians—have learned it is more sophisticated—actually useful—not to "interfere" with colorful local customs.

For example, there is a jail in Jahbad that for sixteen years has housed ten male students who once dared to publicly protest the country's inadequate educational system. They all sit there now: colorful, local lunatics.

Even I was thoroughly charmed by the tall Pathan relative from the Hindu Kush, who came all the way down to Jahbad to meet his first American woman: me. He let me play with his homemade rifle, his bandolier, his turban. His eyes were gentle. He had a smiling bald head. Everyone agreed he was a good man. For example: when his brother had died, he treated his nephews as his own sons, married his sister-in-law—and locked her away for fifteen years. One morning she was found dead. She had hanged herself with a turban. A colorful, local turban.

Oh, the women of Iranistan. The women of the Moslem world. I was no feminist—but now, thinking back, I see how much I might have learned there, how clearly their condition taught me to see: their utter conservatism, their gentle submissiveness, their cruel treatment of female servants and daughters-in-law, their lack of romantic illusions. They taught me about women everywhere. Only because I survived the education can I tell you a few tales of men and women in Iranistan.

Jahbad Maternity Hospital: the corridors and courtyards of this long, low series of wooden buildings remind me of nineteenth-century Russia—a kerchiefed woman slapping a sheet to wash, a samovar in the doctor's private waiting room. A man, wearing a turban and a long quilted coat, is pacing barefoot, back and forth. The doctor, educated in Germany, greets *us* first—then turns to the man and speaks brusquely, with annoyance: "You brought your wife here too late. The baby is already dead. Your wife—not long, maybe a few hours more." Turning back to us, his guests, he offers us tea. "These provincials always come when it's too late." The man has resumed his pacing; the doctor is stirring his sugar. Suddenly the man is yelling, the doctor yelling back.

"Ibrahim," I ask, "should we offer him some money? Can we help?" They are all talking too rapidly for my beginner's Persian. Quietly, Ibrahim translates for me: the man is refusing to pay any hospital fees because not only will he have to pay for his wife's and child's burial, he *now* has to buy another wife to cook for him and take care of the other children. And where, in the name of Allah, did the doctor think he'd be able to get that kind of money? He already had to pay for a car to transport his wife all the way from their village. . . .

I left the hospital as quickly as I could. I didn't want to hear the doctor superciliously dismiss the man's "backward, peasant" behavior; I didn't want to hear the screams of women as we sipped our civilized tea. Now, on the way out, the smell of blood—local and colorful—was unmistakable on some of the drying sheets.

AND WHAT OF IBRAHIM?

Black sheets of women are huddling together at the back of a bus. I laugh out loud in disbelief and nervousness. Two men stare at me.

After two months, I have escaped my polite house arrest, but after two hours of wandering around, I've had enough. I'm lost, I'm frightened, I'm thirsty. Ibrahim was just leaving the family office. He was surprised and embarrassed to see me. "Is anything wrong?" he asked.

"I just wanted to see the city. Ibrahim, can we take a walk, or have lunch somewhere by ourselves? We haven't been alone since we've come here."

The new American restaurant in Jahbad: a cafeteria that serves plastic apple pie and institutional string beans.

Ibrahim won't eat. He has seated us where "they won't see us." His foot taps desperately under the table.

"Ibrahim, I don't know you anymore. Whoever you were, whoever I was—I can't live like this. We have to move out. We have to live by ourselves. . . ."

"How can we do that when you run around the city like this?" he explodes. "Do you know how to handle servants? They'd steal the house, brick by brick. They'd move into our bedroom. They'd sell your underwear. You'd ruin us with parties, with your dancing and drinking. . . . Don't you understand? These people aren't used to such things. They wouldn't understand it. The men will talk. . . ."

"Ibrahim, who have *you* been talking to? You know I don't drink or give wild parties. You can't believe that's really the issue. We can't spend our lives falling asleep over our tea with the terrorized and the idiotic. What will these men really take the wrong way? That I want to be alone with you in our own house? That I want to work? That I don't enjoy being locked up all day with a bunch of frightened women?"

"Who's locking you up, you crazy bitch? Those women are

happier than you'll ever be. . . . Look, look: things are going to change here. But I have to be especially careful. Everyone's watching me, waiting for me to make a slip, to lose my temper, to criticize something. But I won't. No matter what it takes, I've got to be part of changing this country. Someday, if you don't ruin it, I'll be able to do something real here. Then you'll have plenty to do besides being 'locked up.' I'll need you—to teach, to explain, to help me."

"Ibrahim, let's not compare the 'East' and the 'West.' Let's talk about just *us*. Why didn't you ever tell me that your mother is crazy, that you hate your brothers, that you're all afraid of your father, that you're under suspicion for having been away for so long?"

"I'm needed here," Ibrahim answered. "That's why I need you: to help me, to remind me, to give me strength. Please trust me. No one else will."

We were both quiet for a long time. Ibrahim's mouth was pulled down. His eyes were closed. I would have liked to comfort him, but what could I say? Whom would I find myself talking to? He was a stranger.

Winter descends on central Asia without mercy. Already the nights are unbearably cold. I was lying awake on the roof of the world, when I heard a chorus of growls. From my bedroom window I could see the five dogs—dirty, starving mongrels. They had somehow gotten over the wall and had cornered Lara, our pet, a crippled deer. They were eating her alive, gnawing frantically on one hind leg. I ran down. The dogs howled and drew back, their eyes gleaming in fear and hatred. She lay in a twisted heap, death filming her large eyes. One whole leg had been chewed to the bone: it lay exposed under the stars, a dull white. Lights flashed on in the house. *"Che-as?"* [What is it?]. The dogs turned round and round, then sprang into the darkness. I slit her throat with a kitchen knife. . . . A sleepy, frightened gate watchman begged pardon of everyone.

I have fainted for the first time in my life. I'm bedridden with hepatitis—as muddy yellow as the lemons I suck to appease the nausea. I dream of pumpkin pie, ice cream, thick broiled steaks, chocolate cake, but can eat nothing. Yesterday I crawled into the bathroom to throw up, and noticed a new *National Geographic*. The cover story was about the Hunzas, with their long and happy life—nearby. I looked at the photograph of the Himalayans, then saw them again through the bathroom window. Huddled on the floor, I laugh with idiot anguish. I am leading an exotic and adventurous life.

Last week, I crawled downstairs on my hands and knees to find something, anything, to eat, hysterical with hunger. It was late afternoon and no one was around. I met Ali, on his way out to visit his fiancée. I begged for some food. A potato? Some yoghurt? Ali told me, in French, that he hadn't time to look for any food. Zamarut had just fired the new cook. He was already late. . . . Ali paused. "I don't understand how Ibrahim could have brought you here. I've told him that many times."

Jahbad is hidden in snow. In three days, a Russian plane is expected from the Middle East, on its way to Moscow. The doctor at the Tom Dooley hospital has given me a pair of dark glasses to hide my jaundiced eyes. A woman friend has procured an illegal passport for me. My parents have agreed to pay for the flight. My escape is ready—when Abdul Mohammed brings me an Irani passport with a six-month visa granted for "reasons of health."

"Here is your plane ticket. It is better that we see you off. It is better this way."

"You bitch. You whore," Ibrahim rages at me as I pack. "It will take years for me to explain how you got out. You *must* return. I *demand* you return."

"Ibrahim, I have no money. Just a plane ticket. Even if I wanted to come back, I couldn't. Your father doesn't want me here. That's why he won't give you any money to give me. . . ."

Cruel blows. Cruel words. I feel nothing. I feel nothing—until I am flying over hundreds of miles of frozen ice fields toward Tashkent. Light, fierce joy. I am free to begin again.

Jahbad, April 1962

I am becoming an important man, but to my own wife I am nothing, a brown fly, an insect.

Divorce? I see you in a witness box, holding a bouquet of dead roses, telling the judge, the thrill-seeking spectators, the newspapers, all the intimate details of our marriage. Why do you want a part in so horrible a drama?

Jahbad, July 1962

I have decided to tell you everything. You must have a totally clear picture in order to understand what happened to us. Before we arrived in Jahbad, my father had decided that we must live with the family, in order that you learn about the way of life here in the worst way, but in the safest way. This is why he never agreed to help me build or rent my own house. I always lied to you when I said *I* thought it was best for us to live in the family compound.

I lied to you to avoid any conflict between you and my father. I lied because I didn't want you to suffer any hardship. At least we had a roof and food where we were. Just as I was beginning to get established, you became ill. I didn't know what to do, where to turn, how to solve the problem. My father wouldn't budge. . . . Then, over my protest, you insisted on going back to the States. My father took advantage of your insistence.

I took your last letter and went for a man-to-man talk with my father. I asked him to help me, to give me money. . . . He flatly and strongly and definitely refused to do this. I lost control of myself and had a fight with him. As a result, he has just about disowned me. Although we were not on good terms and seldom spoke to each other, now everything is finished. . . .

3. MEN AT SCHOOL

February 1962. Iranistan seems very far away. The College Coffee Shop. In he comes, The Barefoot Boy, as if newly arisen from a bed of dew, in an agony of summoned grace. Dionysius in Passing. Last year he wore pennies in his loafer-heart and drove his father's car at fast sadistic speeds up and down one of our two coasts. How long before some Organization shoes him again? In come The Leather Jackets, riders of a wild, imaginary wind. Only now do I see their pretentiousness, their squinting-through-a-sandstorm gaze, for the innocence, the awkwardness it really is. Only a year ago I thought these boys gods.

The cemetery on campus. Teachers and widows—like Victorian servants who stayed on too long, and have no other place to go—are buried here. Their fringed piano shawls, their European editions, their suede-patched jackets—all, all gather dust in some other place.

Our classrooms are Saxon castles covered with ivy: a dream of Olde and Merrie England on the Hudson. Our classrooms are filled with theatrical male voices, standing left of fireplace, imaginary sherry in hand, declaiming, declaring, proclaiming their sense of failure away in deep Shakespearean rhythms. Straddling the tiny academic globe, in melodious, booming, disembodied voices, they lull us into passivity. We are meant to forget Caesar's power: the mushroom clouds of war.

Professor Rousseau wears a beret. The eternal beret of the professor-rake turning middle-aged, the compulsively unsatisfied satyr. The Middle-Aged Wearing of the Beret: nostalgia for a rebellious Parisian exile never lived? The revolutionary bookseller? The Public School Master as Seducer?

March 1962. Academic men: secular rabbis, scholar-husbands, pretenders to the throne of enlightenment and wealth; they arrive with the wives of the shining hair, the splendid bosom, the gourmet dinner, the wealthy father. Suzanna, for example, of the cream-blond skin and pure gray eyes. Together, we read Proust. She decided to command intellectual attention as a ravishing hostess. Her father would make Italian sabbaticals very comfortable.

What happened to her? Has she already become one of the hollow-eyed faculty wives, overtalkative or oversilent, terrorized by the crop of young, intense, intellectual girls who come and are harvested each year by their professor-husbands? Or has she turned lean with tennis, efficient with children, indispensable with patience? Academic men don't leave this kind of wife for at least twenty years. . . .

That's when they start wearing berets, doing pushups, canceling their classes, and ringmastering sexual orgies or political rallies for their students.

It is just becoming clear to them that they, too, must die.

April 1962. I am lost. I tell our campus philosopher so, and he, the wisest man on campus, tells me, "Have an affair."

But Proust describes me: "Diana—springing from the loins of money changers."

Baudelaire instructs me: "There are two choices open to man to escape the imminent sense of death: pleasure and work. The difference between these two is that one weakens and the other strengthens."

Durrell reminds me:

> I spoke of the uselessness of art but added nothing truthful about its consolations . . . only *there* . . . can reality be re-ordered, re-worked and made to show its significant side . . . for us artists there waits the joyous compromise through art with all that wounded or defeated us in daily life . . .
>
> For those of us who feel deeply and who are at all conscious of the inextricable tangle of human thought, there is only one response to be made—ironic tenderness and silence.

May 1962. The semester is over. Everyone's left, rolled up their posters and madras hangings, packed away the half-finished sculptures and books, the worn-out records—like childhood toys.

Summer. Reluctantly I leave the academic countryside for the Brooklyn of my childhood. Everything is smaller than before: huge cathedrals have become toy churches; massive school years are only small brick buildings. The dead, the bitter ethnic salt of the industrial earth, still sit on their front stoops and porches.

September 1962. "Roberto," I said, "I want to study literature at Yale." "Phyllis, my dear," he said, "that is nothing, nothing at all. Come with me tonight; we'll have a drink with Yevtushenko—you know his work? And we'll arrange everything." I, with my white-floured face, my long black braids, my full breasts and my tiny waist, go to collect my fellowship. "Travel, parties—even *magazine* assignments—that's what she wants," he said, teasing me, stroking my arm.

Roberto, my teacher for three lovely years. We talked Chaucer and Rabelais, Cervantes and Montaigne. Now you're chasing me around the coffee table, around the bed, around the whole damn apartment, until, out of patience and breath, you start yelling:

"You bitch. You tease. You'll never get to Yale if I can help it."

And I didn't. One other true story and you'll know why I've never picked men who could "help" me.

October 1962. "I would never victimize you, never accept any gift you didn't want to give," the famous critic from Europe said, putting his arm around me, kissing me on the cheek. "Lightness is all," he said, touching my breast lightly. "I can give you a great deal. I am at my best in intimacy," he said, touching my thigh intimately. "There is a decision: should my limited amount of energy be spent here? There is only to say 'Yes, it must be,' or 'No, it is quite impossible.' "

And shall we continue talking this way as we lie down together? And afterward, not notice the unmade bed, never discuss the exchange: pretend it never happened? Is this how I would get to those parties filled with his rivals, other accomplished men, who would imagine this scene themselves, behind their clever words?

Must I deliver myself to the Centaur *shyly?* Why must Centaurs bother with seduction? Don't they know that if I am moved, I will appear at their door one evening, more eager than they are for our exchange of energies?

Ah, the academics are so tired, so obsessed with victory and death. They need to rest, to escape, to win false victories—with women. And I ask so many questions, they'd never get any sleep, they'd be annoyed by the cruelty of my ambition: they'd never tell me much.

But mainly, they're no longer beautiful nor forbidden. Hard to find a Tiresias who is.

4. MEN IN NEW YORK CITY

November 1962. There is less sky in Manhattan. Here, our steel reach to heaven has made men small and interchangeable; has blotted out the stars, and with them, the binding relief of perspective; our common humanity. Our souls, our bodies, are being narrowed and elongated to match the elongation of the architecture. Women wear green nail polish and silver shoes, to match green-glass and silver-steel buildings. A multitude of human intentions—and all reach the same, sharp, insolent skyline peak. Yet what a fairyland it is, on postcards and in dreams.

Today, I rode the Fifth Avenue bus from Fifty-seventh Street down to Eighth Street, falling asleep against the great glass curve of the window. A fine rain, almost white, woke me, softening everything. When it rains, Manhattan becomes more like a European city to me. Rain—in soft sheets, even in cold, hard clatters—changes the city. Rain softens all our sharp edges, it slows our movements, it provides the city with a common obstacle to overcome: a transient hint of community.

Today, I saw a boy from my high school class disguised as a repairman for Con Edison. "Oh, is *that* who he is!" Is that what it's all about! When you see your own age in adult uniform, instantly you see the tenuousness, the sad inevitability of the mating: the man to the job, the fear to the defense. My schoolmates have already become the butchers, the bakers—the repairmen of cities.

February 1963. My college years over, gone, fled away six months ago. Greenwich Village. Male backs bend forward over tables, listening, not to interpretations of the universe, not to declarations of suicide, but to deals: money-deals, music-deals, political-deals, dope-deals. I sip cappuccino at the tiny Italian café that alone remains unchanged.

March 1963. In the sauna. Dull white human beings sitting with blank and listless faces. Only the droplets of sweat at hairline and throat seem thoughtful. Here sexuality—a hint of something subtle or personal—is submerged among the many repetitions of breast and thigh and belly.

Sweating, I realize the danger of mass nudity: mass human expendability. The women here are not "themselves": they are more like each other. I understand why soldiers are made to strip and shower together; why naked prisoners, naked slaves, naked Jews, naked women can excite such brutality and such amnesia.

May 1963. Waiting for a bus to Newark at the Port Authority Bus Terminal. The radio says: "A mad-dog killer of women has escaped from his hospital prison." I stand there, surrounded by sailors, winos, and commuters from New Jersey; I could easily become one of the killer's next hostages or victims.

Housewives in hair curlers will switch off soap operas to discuss, in detail, the details about his latest victim. The movie based on the book will capture, in grainy black-and-white, the portrait of an America that still remembers breadlines and lynchings with nostalgia. The American male who reads the *National Enquirer* imagines a whore in every chicken pot and spills his seed in movie houses all over the buttered popcorn. The announcement of the arrival of my bus startles me back into fantasy.

October 1963. I went to a Times Square movie this Monday afternoon to see a Swedish film about the "futility of rehabilitating juvenile delinquents." I sat surrounded by men who had come to see a film about a "girl forced into an unnatural sex act with a dog." There they all sat, spaced out in their overcoats: the unemployed, the unemployable, night workers, civil servants, businessmen with scarves and briefcases, salesmen "catching a few hours."

My God: Do we really think we won't have another and another and yet another war? Such lust, such self-hate, such restlessness, *must be satisfied.* I think these men are more interested in violent wars than in pornographic films.

September 1963. At the burlesque. Fat men. Bald men. Poor men. Jerking off together the way they once did as kids. Communion. Men-children, yelling out their private "come-words," having them bounced right back into their laps. "That's it, work out, baby. Move that ass . . . ahh." "Work out": is it an athlete they fantasy in this tasseled tease of a place? It's true: men can never walk down aisles as the brides of football heroes. Men won't have their hearts broken (again) by Daddy. That's woman's work.

On the street. Men and women dress in "costumes"—outfits fashioned from every historical period and borrowed from every part of the globe. Cowboys and Indians, Space-Astronaut Girls, Frontier Grannies, Parisian Élégantes—all pass each other, all meet themselves on the street. Quick-change artists, reliving the past, looking for some road not taken, some escape route. Carnival time, as Rome burns slowly—but more brightly than the last time.

November 22, 1963. Dallas, Texas, on New York television. Old, bald heads walked in a confusion of dignity—retired spirits suddenly called to recognize youth's desertion of the future. These men, already thrown over by history, marched in Washington today. A double assassination, a Father-killing, a Son-killing. To all of us, Kennedy was both—and is dead. The country will never quite recover. The country will not understand it for years.

Christmas Eve, 1963. In the lap of the archetype, two European shoemakers are working. A woman with a small boy comes in. Roughly, she pushes her son up into a shoeshine seat, puts on her husband's apron, and starts to polish the child's shoes. It is lovely, sexual adoration. The boy squirms with power and delight, one moment a trapped infant, the next a young, commanding adolescent. Tapping, the father speaks gruff love words to the boy. The woman is silent. The child becomes silent. Outside, on East Seventy-ninth Street, it is dusk and smells improbably of pine trees.

5. MEN AT WORK

The Brain Research Laboratory, May 1966. Steve, my boss, is in his mid-forties, virile, magnetic, deadly. In working-class clothes, he sits beneath pictures of Einstein and Marx. He speaks genially to offices in Washington: quite at home in the glacial corporate age. His laboratory is, not coincidentally, staffed by "underlings" : male students who will never finish their dissertations; European physicians who cannot practice medicine in America; faithful Asian technicians—all female—who do exactly as they're told.

I work hard, learn fast, and become the only "independent" spirit for him to challenge, intimidate, overlook—and secretly respect. I was the only one—ever—to finish a Ph.D dissertation in his laboratory, his castle, his kingdom.

In the laboratory, Steve *fucks* each delicate electrode as he makes it, pelvis thrust forward, as if he's jackhammering away at some construction site.

America's scientists are fascists, taking reality by storm, by force—for ideologies' sake. Upstairs, in Neurophysiology, I've noticed that the Chairman always wants to be informed when the "acute preparation"—a dog or cat—must remain unanesthetized. He always stops by—a sergeant, overlooking the interrogation of a prisoner.

John and Aaron: my colleagues. For them this lab is a teenager's room, filled with a dozen half-finished experiments, each one started in a burst of love and left aside when a new and even more startling thought occurs to either of them. Steve is not the mother to clean up after them. He talks to them like a father: bitingly, contemptuously, threateningly. Their lack of discipline, their inability to "deal" with authority both pleases and enrages him.

Each month, one of the "boys" is fired—or quits. Angry words, door-slamming, desks being emptied—and at dawn, John (or Aaron) is exhausted, forlorn, regretful. Over coffee in the hospital cafeteria, he gets the best idea he's had yet and stays for the rest of the day. Good thing too: we couldn't find half the equipment in the lab without these two half-geniuses. They ordered, or built, most of what's here, while Steve was running around to get the money to pay for it.

April 1967. One day Aaron is found at an airport trying to pilot a passenger plane to Heaven. Hospitalized, he grew fat on tranquilizers and candy. Afterward, back at the lab, Aaron sat listlessly at his desk, or at someone else's, fiddled with computer dials, stopped talking in midsentence. He told me he was really a poet, not a scientist. One day, Aaron went to his mother's house, slit his throat in the kitchen, and died. He is never mentioned at the lab.

Summer, 1967. Scientists. When a new machine—a computer, for example—is delivered, all other work stops. The men crowd around "her" as if it's a girl they've just given birth to, as if it's a girl they're all going to fuck, as if it's a million-dollar baby. (It is.) The men who get excited are safer than the silent ones. The icy loners. The deadly constipates. The men in white socks with no chins and neatly bulging briefcases, who present their findings as imperious victory speeches, or in paranoid monotones, to a male audience waiting to attack—or lick ass.

Sven in research. 1967. The hospital's best electron microscopist is from Finland. His only demand had been for an experienced Swedish female technician. He got one: as gaunt and willing as her mother and her grandmother were before her. All day, her thoughts hummed together as she clattered about in the lab, preparing the doctor's slides and lunch with equal care, equal craft. Eventually, she yielded to his loneliness with an old-fashioned abandon and the same efficiency (afterward, sandwiches and a remade bed) that made her laboratory work so valuable.

Then one morning, in her thirty-fifth year, she told him she was pregnant. Her stubbornly long figure bent farther into her microscope. The silence lengthened over them like a late afternoon thought. She began to cry. "So this is woman," Sven thought, slightly pleased, slightly awed. They were married in her fourth month.

Thoughtful, deeper in stride, Sven spent full days of work in New York, his wife at his side, his briefcase bulging at night with the papers and photographs she'd packed for him to scrutinize before he shut off the light over their bed to listen for a while to the clock and his wife's steady breathing in the darkness. Early Sunday mornings, they walked, in European slow motion, through Central Park.

Sometimes we would join them for dinner. On those evenings, Sven made a show of lighting the centerpiece candle. He cleared his throat. He adjusted his chair. He read the menu out loud, considering and rejecting each item until his usual choice was rediscovered. And then he strained forward to hurry its beginning, the conversation that warmed and excited him, a more intense form of energy he'd long known existed, a laughing

Grushenka waiting for him in a troika at some border of his ice-silenced country.

"Ah, yes, ah, no," he would exclaim, his shy clarity already seduced, made girlish, by his expectations. His friends seemed to discuss everything. Even affairs of the heart contained as many devious, invisible determinants, as did the chromosomes he studied. By midevening, his wit found its way into words. Ideas pulsed in his throat, and at his temples. He copied the names of two "journals of opinion" into his notebook. He civilized his pleasure into questions. He became drunk on words, more hopelessly so than he used to be on whiskey at the Finnish students' drinking bouts.

The doctor's wife sat quietly during these conversations, like one of those unpretty little girls who silence their mother's murderous impulses with obedience and aggressive self-sufficiency. She listened to her belly swelling. She trapped her yawns between her long, timid knees. And she waited to go home. At the end of her seventh month, she refused to attend these dinners. "The politics so upset the baby," she cried in her round, lilting English.

Sven began to drink. His wife refused to return to work as his assistant. He began to beat her. She nearly miscarried—but gave birth to a son a little early.

The doctor's work was not the same. He wasn't fulfilling his promise. The department chairman—a self-made millionaire, a prizewinner, didn't have much patience with men who were so vulnerable to women. Sven would have to go. Let him find his own equipment in Finland.

Now, whatever happens, it will first go on like this for a long time. It is probably something Strindberg on Marriage, or Tolstoy, in *The Kreutzer Sonata,* would understand.

The Hospital. January 1968. My year of internship. If I ever get hit by a bus, I've got a card in my wallet listing the hospitals I *don't* want to be taken to. It's the Welfare Department all over again, but *this* is the place they cart the welfare clients off to when they go berserk in the caseworker's office, or when they're mugged, knifed, or raped on the street. Here is where people come to sit, for hours, for days, to get eyeglasses, false teeth, and hysterectomies. *Here* is where people get experimented on for the sake of "science," for the sake of scientists' careers, for the sake of other, paying patients in private rooms.

Physician-scientists. My colleagues have implanted electrodes in the lateral geniculate of a young woman with a terminal case of brain cancer. The implantation ceremony was "unofficial," and the doctors had to extract the electrodes hurriedly, just before she died. As the experimenters stood around her bed, after they'd finished flashing a light in her eyes and recording responses, a single tear drizzled down her cheek. Outside, her young husband sat in the corridor, waiting for her to die.

The neurology ward: the patients are comatose. They cannot hear the blare of the nurse's radio; they cannot see that the doctors aren't there; they cannot answer the social worker's questions. She checks off "no response" to each one. A kid named Bobby Rice is in bed, his skull top unlatched for a freshman anatomy lecture, leering at me. Rice was driving with his friends at a hundred miles an hour when he crashed through his nervous system into this Ward. For twenty-one days he whirred along—a hooked-up mechanical grotesque—until one afternoon his mother, upon arriving, found another boy—not her son—in her son's bed. No one told her he died last night.

For a while, I used to see Rice jerk by me on the street, a stocking cap over his brain puddle, carrying his own lifesaving equipment, waving hello.

The narcotics ward. I see psychiatrists inject the experimental patients with the purest of heroin, to measure "brain waves and sexual attitudes under the influence of . . ." The doctors grow *aroused* watching these presumed studs and pimps and muggers turn into the impotent, dependent children they really are. In turn, the doctors turn genial—almost paternal—with relief that they are so unlike these ghetto gamesters, these smiling prisoners.

Doomed junkies in cotton undershirts beg the doctors to be in this particular experiment.

The ward. Luis, a "patient" with a black turtleneck smile. Luis, I lust after you, for your warm, slow, cruel infancy, for your 3-minute, 45 rpm machismo. Once, Luis explained to his friend why a fifteen-year-old girl "got crazy" for him. "Man," says Luis, "it's nothing personal. She just opened up, like a flower. I just happened to be there when the sun came up and she was ready to go."

The ward philosopher. The handsomest con man there.

One Hundred and Seventeenth Street is a page out of *Naked Lunch,* a carnival of junkies and pushers in electric green and purple, all milling, shuffling, hustling on the street, shooting crap on the stoop. My "patients" wave and smile at me from behind double-parked Cadillacs.

Juan is embarrassed to find me waiting for him. (Twice now I've gotten him out of jail.) His arms are loaded down with goods just stolen. Hot from someone's apartment. He insists on buying me coffee and some very greasy Spanish food. What the hell am I doing here? White Boss Broad with her basket of liberal roses. In group therapy sessions, I talk about revolution and music, and they're polite. They don't laugh out loud, or get nasty. They just sit there imagining how really revolutionary it would be if I got them heroin, gave them money, or whored for them. Later on, when I won't, they call me "cunt" and feel betrayed. They really *need* the money.

Doctors not at work ski the Alps, play golf in country clubs, shoot the rapids in Colorado, attend opening nights on Broadway. Some doctors, when they're not at work, pretend to be men of independent wealth. Lawrence, the internist, for example. Each month we're invited to dinner. (*We're* invited. I go along with a male physician. Women colleagues are never there

—unless they're the wives of Department Chairmen.) Lawrence serves me fresh and glistening cheese himself. At my service. The room is filled with physicians.

They talk of paintings, real estate, art, and good years for wine. They also talk of whom to trust, or whom to fear. They speak of whom they'd like to work for. After dinner, thick green Havana cigars, brandy, coffee poured from a silver service. The wives are all young, but already know how to manage servants, are already in touch with the best private schools, already know where the best vacations can be had.

Less than ten blocks away, the poor are propped up in several hospital emergency rooms; a patient rings for a nurse who doesn't answer; an ambulance arrives too late; a young intern, without sleep for two days, doesn't know what to do.

Apologia. For at least twelve long years these physicians as students have been goaded by ambition, by parents, by competitors, and by sadistic professors, into forgoing "life" in order to learn to save it. "I'll make them pay," they mutter, long-distance runners, biding their time. And the patients do "pay": in money, in respect, in dependency.

But even the money is not enough. The burden of battling poverty and death is staggering. Each day death triumphs; each day more patients insist that doctors know what to do; each day there are more patients. This unhinges all but the gentlest of healers, the saints, the exceptions. Most doctors withdraw, turn cold and contemptuous: a child's most frightening tantrum.

6. MEN AT HOME

1963–1966. David. When I first saw David, he was wearing a trench coat, overly belted and overly flared: a sign of something feminine, something daring, something insecure. In bed, the woman in him proclaims herself in a gently tapered ankle and in how lovingly he loves me. Especially, she is there in how patiently he teaches me all about Science. And when he sings lover's songs from Spain and Greece on his guitar.

Ah, how the woman in him makes him suffer! How she stubbornly refuses to run with the other boys. Like his mother, David prefers to stay at home: with his books, his dreams, his music—and with me.

David. I was happy living with him. Conversations at breakfast, conversations at dinner: between father and daughter, between father and son—sometimes, even, between mother and child. I had all the right combinations, except I forgot that I can't stay home. And that I can't return there either.

One evening, I looked up from my book and knew that this

could go on forever, that I might never run away again. And so I leave.

David. For years afterward, we exchange poems and midnight telephone calls, discuss our lovers, our jobs, his melancholy, my "progress." Slowly, things change.

Now David publishes scientific papers. I know, because when we meet, he is, more and more often, always to the point. He has lost his hair (those brown, brown curls). He begins to choose women whom he doesn't like—who know him as testy, difficult, demanding.

My David. Now, he never drives without wearing a seat belt, without tensing up over the road map before he starts the engine. He keeps antacid pills in the glove compartment and demands them, pointing, his eyes never leaving the road ahead. David has also left our home, to go to meet his death. Now, he is doing what you "have" to do.

Enough of finding the same past and future skull beneath each man's face. Now I will know men only as brothers and as sons.

1966–1969. But for Harold. I found my mother in this sternly beautiful physician astride a ballet-horse: Lucifer, alone, in search of me, fleeing. In the wilderness of sexual deceit, Harold, a Jewish Prince is searching for his Father. He looks for him in women, but never finds him there. Always he is fooled, disappointed, haunted by these Fathers who turn into Mothers: like me, like me, they are all dumbly eager to please, hysterical with grief, darkly abandoned. Like his own mother, abandoned by her husband who died when Harold was six years old.

Tenderly Harold holds his past to himself, "rewarding" me with bits and pieces of it when I've been especially "fatherly," that is, detached, distant, preoccupied. He tells me about Virgil Thomson and Edward Albee and William Flanagan—and reverently, obliquely, about his dead "friend" Leon, the music critic. I imagine them lovers. I imagine that Harold picks up men in

Central Park, in subway stations, at the riding academy. I am wrong. (Years later, smoking dope in California with a Harold turned hippie, he tells me that he never slept with another man, he had only pretended to. The first time was two months ago, and he couldn't come.)

When Harold gets angry, he attacks me with Silence. The sight of an unfilled radiator pan in our bedroom, the thought that it might dry up before morning, convinces him that I want to deprive him of oxygen. He asks me if *I'd* like to be choked. I apologize. I joke. I move toward him with nervous affection.

Harold becomes hysterical, demands a *complete answer,* mimics my "wide-eyed innocence." Then he withdraws behind his newspaper to be "left alone," in domestic peace; he contemplates a proper "punishment." I fill and refill the bedroom radiator pan until it overflows; I want it to slosh over his feet, a room away! As always, Harold sleeps soundly—and wakes me at six A.M. by loudly running and rerunning water in the bathtub. My punishment: he hides my lipstick, my lab notes, a poem I've written, under the couch. And he won't tell me where they are. He's not "talking" to me.

The longest silent treatment was nearly thirty days. I ask Harold's best friend to please stop living with us and go home to his wife, his girlfriend, or his mother. The casual presence of their intense and complicated companionship is more than I can live with. For two months, I watch it strengthen daily—almost in response to my discomfort, my envy, my female child's face pressed to the window of their unspoken "arrangement." I see only what's always existed: two men who need each other, who *prefer* each other to women, but who won't, who can't say so. I see they want *me* to solve their dilemma with my (mother's) body and my (father's) understanding. They want my parental blessing.

And will we live together, we three, finding our sexual partners elsewhere, each of us protecting the other two from the demands of strange and beautiful girls? As long as I sing over the cooking, they'll gladly remember to bring home overpriced Chinese and Italian dinners to go.

Ah! Does Harold realize he is not "there" for me—is that it? Has he brought another home to make up for it, to keep me there, or to keep his friend, to have us both, to have everything? Oh, the combined needs of these two men, these two Jews in exile! "Milton," I say, "I think you'd better go for now." "Phyllis, you're right, but be careful with Harold, explain it carefully."

My punishment: suddenly, Harold *accuses* me of knowing all along that he's had a mistress twenty years my senior, another five years my junior, a hotel room, and many anonymous sexmates. I persistently *chose* to torture him with my naivete. I have bored him with my innocence and still expect more of him than he wants to give! He doesn't talk to me for that whole month.

When I leave, Harold warns me not to, predicts my regret, describes the dangers and the difficulties, swears not to care about me, refuses me a can opener, a mirror, the extra bed, blocks the doorway, screams after me down the hallway.

As I said, a true mother's words.

Bill. 1968–1969. At the Brain Research Lab. How completely this shy and quiet mathematician appeased my hundred questions with his lips, his hands, his body—so white and smooth of skin, so sensual for so serious a Methodist. We made love every day, everywhere: on his sailboat, beneath cold night stars; in his wife's bed when she was away on business; in my bed when Harold was away at work; and always, in the lab. One of us would push our back against the door, to block anyone who might want to watch our experiment that day.

Bill cried when I said, "This isn't enough—you only want to sail red balloons in the park with me. Sunday nights, Christmas Eve, when everyone's home with their family, so are you."

"Oh," he said, "this is different from what I have at home." Sadly, prophetically, he said, "It's more—it's different from what you ever have at home." Ah, Bill, you wistful sunchild, you dreamer, you Father-abandoned child, you were right.

Sex like ours, without "love," going nowhere because it has already arrived; such intense sex with friendship is certainly a form of love not found at home. Why not leave yours, then, Bill? Or is there something to a home that I, too, should have?

1970

John

sweaty
with egotism and alcohol,
you played honky-tonk piano for me
in your lumberjack boots,
and cooked us midnight supper
as if we lived in Paris
in 1905 in an opera.

Trouble was,
I wasn't thin enough or mad.
I refused to cut my wrists,
I refused to sell your secrets to the police for compliments,
I refused the drowning artist his seaweed-death:
coin for shelter with his married friends.
Where would I get it? I was no mermaid.

Trouble was,
you didn't like how much your songs
charmed Hell out of me.

Trouble was—well, that
there wasn't enough of it.

1970

Arthur

All adroop—walrus mustache, shoulders, Jewish eyes—
you mourned your life at me:
you'd been down so long
that to surface now
would be a form of suicide.
(like burning your books and your skin
fighting in Sinai).

But it turned you on that I wanted to be Robert Redford
(in any of his films).
There were times we laughed too fast to fuck things up.

Trouble was,
I wasn't jealous
(you sulked alot over that one),
and I worked mornings
(you tried to end that, fought nights with me).

Trouble was,
when you wouldn't suck me
(your mother hadn't left the house in 10 years),
I put my fist through the window—
or would have if I wasn't a girl,
and stopped talking to you.

1970

Ronald

You arrived suddenly, with a suitcase and a tale of woe:
a little tall for Greta Garbo,
a little old for Ophelia
(but still ten years my Junior).
I let you in,

thought you'd make off with my only bottle of perfume
and marry the boy next door.

Trouble was,
you stayed,
and once, with tears on your lashes,
made perfect young love to me.
Somehow
you became my temporary Black Prince.

Trouble was,
you left:
a classic case of sons and lovers.

1970

Allen

You seemed a jerk
until you told me to spend my summer in a convent.
After that, I chanced upon our conversation
as upon an Enchanted Forest
(I the deer, you the hunter,
I the jester's shadow, you the hangman).
Oh, it was very medieval.

Trouble was,
I was the first Jewish girl you'd ever slept with
—after two WASP wives.
(I hadn't a chance.)
Look: you'd tried to turn me Catholic
before you'd even kissed me.

1970

Faisal

From the least likely quarter—an old and native one for me—
understanding.

In your clipped and singsong voice,
your brown and double vision,
you seemed a secret childhood playmate come out of hiding.

Trouble was,
we were grounded by your Magic Carpet of words,
and by my sense of violence
(under the bed, at the bottom of the lake, in your every act).

Trouble was—well, that
there was too much of it for me.

1971. Wayne. When we kissed goodbye, merely comrades in the scientific inquiry, I smelled your button-down shirt—and imagined ten such shirts in fresh-smelling, light blue piles of married woman's love. Suddenly I wanted it: a room with a fireplace, a dog, skis, and a scrapbook of camping trips. I would even enjoy the faculty parties: quiche Lorraine, a little too much to drink, a little too much of too little to say. I was kissing your absent wife Laurie in you and didn't realize I yearned for what she gave you, not what you gave her.

Wayne. Married at nineteen, you took my challenge and left Laurie, the dogs, the house, the university—to rebuild them all over again with me. (A more "interesting" woman, a "fellow" Ph.D., a professor, a writer, a divinely obsessed feminist.) Did you imagine we'd work together? Or that I'd give up ambition to iron shirts and brew deep and golden health-food tea? How confused, how cheated you must have felt, to wake up at every campsite, to find me already surrounded by papers and books, absently smiling you away to a day in the wilderness, alone.

Wayne. You, of the slender hipbones and funny, warm gloves and socks—you taught me to climb mountains. I am grateful forever. But when you saw how poorly I took orders, how poorly I rowed kayaks and repacked bedrolls; when you realized that your "good behavior" would have to last forever: with me, there was never any pardon or release from the asylum of equality. Ah, then you turned cruel, short-tempered, and boasted of your sexual freedom.

Years later, in Toronto, after a lecture, Laurie of the laundered shirts, wearing long, long braids, leapt up onto my lecture stage, and kissed me. I, finally, kissed her too. "Why couldn't *you* have taught me to climb mountains?" I asked. "Do women never learn that from each other?"

And what news of you? Laurie shook her head and said, "Oh, him. Now he's living with a girl half his age who cooks very fragrant rice dishes, makes very fragrant candles at home, and never says anything."

1971. Mark. Incredible Sundays in "real" America. Finishing my first book at the MacDowell Colony in New Hampshire. Evergreen firs, red moving hunters, snow flurries at the window, the smell of morning coffee and green apples being baked into dinner-pies. I have known such Sundays only as the lover of Christian men. Men and boys who bring me home for visits to small towns in the Adirondacks, the White Mountains, the Colorado Rockies.

Mark. Blond and sullen, he came from the local town to the artists' colony to find "artists." I think he had men in mind: painters who dress and work like laborers, in concrete, in plastic, with thirty feet of canvas. Father-figures, vindicators, a route out of the matchbox factory in Mark's town. At home, the men laughed at Mark's self-portraits: sad old men who looked like them. They "borrowed" his other portraits of himself: lush women in languorous, pornographic exposure.

Mark. "Mark's like a priest," his mother always said, happy to nurse him through an excessive number of illnesses. His older brothers beat him secretly. His father never spoke much, spent most of his time working, sleeping, and fixing things in the basement with his eldest son.

In the kitchen, Mark's mother and Mary, his younger sister-in-law, ply me with food and questions. In the kitchen where we sit, the women spell out their complaints of loneliness: their husbands never talk to them, their husbands don't enjoy going to church. Their husbands don't enjoy romantic movies on television—they always change it to a game. Mary shows me the bruises from her last beating as proudly as she does her wedding picture and the picture of her backyard picnic and the barbecue pit. "When I have his son," she says, patting her swelling stomach, "there'll be less of that."

Soup simmering, meat roasting, the sound of a clock ticking. Indoors. The smell of women waiting, the smell of female acquiescence drives me outdoors to join the men, drinking beer in ski-doos, in motorcycles, in souped-up cars. They at least move around and make some noise, gunning motors, showing off their shooting rifles, hammering extra rooms onto small houses.

They are playing lord-in-the-woods this Sunday, using this day to stretch and stalk and die out loud—not motionless like their women inside, not motionless like themselves, on factory Monday.

Finally, it is the smell of blood that sends me away. Mark's hair is so long that one day when the police stop him for speeding, they beat him until he is bloody. The town worries too much: only a year later he'll come home; only a year later he'll live on his own in New York, drawing women fucking each other, fucking men, fucking dogs—and Mark, afterward.

PART THREE

AN ESSAY ABOUT MEN

Fathers and Sons

The Oedipal Drama

On Having a Penis

Talking to Men About Sex

Pornography and Other Male Sexual Fantasies

Brotherhood

1. FATHERS AND SONS

What do sons feel and remember about their fathers? From the psychoanalytic point of view, a man's first woman, his mother, is taken from him by his father; and his second woman, the mother of his first son, is taken from him by his son. Not an easy rivalry to live with, and yet an uncanny silence surrounds this drama. Sometimes, the silence is broken by Oedipal claims of omnipotence and revenge—"I've really gotten even with my father. He can't control me at all"; sometimes the silence is broken by emotionally wild expressions of anger and contempt for the mothers and wives involved. Much less often, if at all, do we hear sons pierce the silence with public, verbal accounts of their emotional relationships with their fathers.

It is women, in private settings, who most often share men's memories of having been belittled, criticized, not taken seriously—patronized—by their fathers. Unless men have a reason to praise their fathers, they usually remain silent about them in (male) public.

Upon being questioned, men are mildly and surprisingly amnesiac about what occurred between themselves and their fathers. Some men say:

> "You wanna know about my childhood? Let me tell you about my mother . . . my mother never let me alone for a minute. I had to run away from her, from her *mouth,* to save my life. My father's fists were nothing compared to her words, her tears, her complaints."

Men usually find it hard to tell me much about their fathers. They tell me what kind of work a father did. They tell me whether his life was "hard" or "easy." They tell me what country he came from, and whether he's still alive. (It could be Telemachus trying to imagine what Odysseus was like, or Oedipus, describing his unseen father, Laius.)

Upon being questioned about their fathers, many educated men immediately shift into "theoretical" discourse. "Marx believed," "Freud said," "Obviously Nixon thought," "Research on apes has shown." Anything, anything, is safer, is preferable to talking about themselves in relation to their own fathers.

"Did your father ever beat you?" I'll ask. And in response most men immediately discuss male violence in the abstract, male violence on some other continent, male violence as *other* men practice it on *other* men. Not as they practice it. Not as it was practiced on them.

Sometimes, in a quiet voice, or more often, in tough and realistic tones, a man will tell me:

> "Yes, my father hit me. Yes, I was afraid of him. Yes, I hated him. But I loved him, too. It's all so long ago. And it wasn't his fault that he beat me, drank too much, never came home, died too soon—or always preferred my brother to me."

A twenty-five-year-old said:

> "My father? Man. I hate that guy. He's a loser. A bum. He used to blame it on some business deal that got loused up. I guess he

took it out on my mother. Then he got around to me. He'd beat me up every fucking night if he found me just hanging around the house. . . . My mother blamed it on the whiskey. Not me. I knew him for a vicious punk. I stayed away from home a lot but where could I stay for too long?

"In a way, I feel sorry for the guy. But I wish he was dead. I really do. Whad he ever do for me! Make me cry? Teach me I hadda fight everyone—even my own father?"

No matter how anxious or amnesiac my informants were about paternal physical violence, they were even more anxious, mute, defenseless, when I asked them, "Did your father kiss you?" This question of kisses left most men without even a method of distancing themselves from their feelings. (No one talked about men kissing *other* men on some other continent.) In other words, as I looked for the psychologically "good" aspects of the father-son relationship, I discovered, quite predictably, the same tragedy of lost opportunity that characterizes most mother-daughter relationships. One thirty-year-old man said:

"My father wasn't very affectionate. He was a cold, precise person. . . . I don't remember his hitting me ever. He always griped and complained about whatever I did. I remember when I was four my father was building a garage and he told me it would be dangerous for me to help him. I was too young, too little. That's when I started my first fantasies of being a cripple. Really. I would put on my clothes so that my leg was stuck in my pants and I wished I could wear glasses. . . .

"My mother still kisses me on the lips when I'm leaving. My father shakes hands with me at the train station."

Another man, in his mid-thirties, said:

"I like my father. I guess he's the best kind of person he can be. He's not a very deep-thinking person. He trudges along, does his job, doesn't complain too much. . . .

"I guess I don't really know my father . . . it's very difficult for me to talk to my father. Even now, he gets upset with any idea that isn't a conservative one. He gets red in the face and asks me if I'm a Communist: a real *Daily News* mentality. The guy's got a heart condition. I just don't talk to him about that stuff.

"My father always shook hands with me. As he got older, I began to sort of kiss him goodbye. I don't know exactly what he does. He doesn't kiss me back. I guess he lets me kiss him. That's what he does."

Among men, though, there are crucial and unique advantages to be gained in accepting or "resolving" the father-son relationship. If sons are adequately socialized into patriarchy, they can then "bond" with other men for economic gain. Also, they are prepared, in rejecting identification with their mothers, for a life of "male" work; they are also able to enslave women and other men with only moderate degrees of awareness or guilt. These advantages are not spiritual or emotional ones. Men are not taught how to be interpersonally sensitive to others—or to themselves. Despite male egotism and narcissism, most men tend to lack the emotionally introspective tools that would allow them to comfort others or to comfort themselves. For example, one man, upon being asked about his father's violence, replied:

"Oh. He wasn't ever violent. He left my mother when I was born. He only came back to visit every so often. For about ten years I think."

Stunned, I said, "Don't you think of his abandonment or his nonavailability as an act of violence?"

He responded, without any visible emotion: "Well, I guess you could look at it that way. But I know a lot of guys who probably wish their fathers had stayed away."

Most children in this century, in the Western world, are raised by their mothers, no matter how much money their fathers earn. No matter how many memorable Sunday outings their fathers provided, if I can believe what I have been told, men themselves feel that they have been raised only by their mothers.

A man named Edward made this statement on the subject:

"My father is a gentle man. He was always very shy, very timid, in social situations . . . it's true, now that you're asking about it, my father's life is not as visible to me as my mother's. . . .

"My *grandfather* was the tyrant in the family. He expected me to be good at riding a bicycle and playing football. I can remember being embarrassed because my grandfather was ashamed that I never became an athlete . . . my mother let me take dancing lessons with my sister—ballet and tap. But I could never tell anyone I was doing it. My father seemed proud of me. But I still knew I was doing something shameful or humiliating.

"Theoretically, I think fathers have a great rage against their sons. Sons get a kind of unconditional love from their mothers. Fathers are jealous."

There *are* "good" fathers and "good" mothers; but let us admit, even if the admission angers, frightens, or shames us, that while "good" people do exist, they are a rarity, a miracle, a blessed exception. Unfortunately, the Parents of the human race are not "good" people: not always, not all the time, and not often enough.

It was startling to hear men respond to a variety of questions about their fathers with "sexual" information about themselves. For example, at least twenty men responded to the question, "Tell me about your relationship to your father," by telling me, abruptly, aggressively, defensively—bizarrely—all about "sex." They said: "I'm a highly sexed man," or "I masturbate insatiably," or "I'm pretty sadistic sexually to women—but it turns me on and they have no complaints," or "I'm afraid I might be a homosexual," or "I'm a very happy homosexual, sexually speaking." All this in response to a question about their fathers!

As if they wanted to warn me off this topic. As if the father-son relationship somehow demands a genitally sexual solution—a solution which civilization prohibits.

Afterward, the thought of this strange possibility made me wonder to what extent traditional male homosexuality is related to a desire to solve the psychopolitical war between fathers and sons. Or to a desire on the part of men, especially recently, to defuse the escalation of male-male rivalry by eliminating women as a basis for competition.

Patriarchal civilization is, from one point of view, a male homosexual civilization. Women are valued only for their reproductive capacities. In all other areas, men prefer to remain separate from women, and in close contact with other men. A culture that covets such separatist all-male control of religious, military, economic, and political institutions is, psychologically speaking, a homosexual culture.

Of course, the argument is often made that so rigid a separation of the sexes is an expression of male reverence for or male envy of woman's childbearing capacities. And so it is, as you have seen in the section "Womb-less Men."

As I listened to some of the tapes of my "interviews" with strange men, and as I read my notes over again, certain unlooked-for themes in the father-son relationship *did* emerge. For example: most firstborn sons described having a harder time emotionally with their fathers than did second- and third-born sons.

Here are three typical responses:

> "I have a brother. A younger, adopted brother. He's more like them [my parents]. I don't know why they adopted him . . . maybe they didn't like me. . . ."

> "My younger brother talked back to my father all the time—a real smartass. I felt I would really get to my father by never letting him see anything I was doing. I hid up in my room a lot."

> "My younger brother—I admire him so much. He's the real success in the family. . . . I haven't seen him since World War Two."

Also, the older men I talked to have all either forgotten, forgiven, or so completely repeated their father's paternal patterns that they are not as condemning, not as angry, toward their fathers as are younger men. This may be because there were more realistic expectations about parents at the beginning of the twentieth century. Also, more resigned and sentimental understanding of life among "older" people may account for this difference in tone.

Charles, age fifty, was born in the rural South:

> "My father had family, money, education, and great expectations—to live up to. So: he drank. A great deal. I can assure you I didn't see him much when I was very young. But I didn't see my mother either. They were busy people. I was kept busy. I suppose we only spent time together when I was properly grown up. . . .
>
> "I was never good at books or sports—but I wasn't bad either. You know, a little like my father, a little like my mother, a little like myself. My father—*the family*—were always generous to me. I was introduced to the right people at the right time. I guess I've done the right things in my own life.
>
> "My father died of his drinking. Just about now. I mean at my age. . . . He must have been a lonely man, an insecure man, a man who meant well. I know. Because I am."

Frank, age sixty, was born in Italy:

> "My father—he was a farmer, a laborer, a merchant marine. Sure—he hit me. He had to. I was a wild kid. Couldn't speak English, couldn't even read Italian. I was used to going around barefoot, stealing fruit and chickens from the rich neighbor. . . . This was America. I had to help my mother take care of my sisters, go to school, earn some money too. . . . He didn't do bad by me. I can't complain. I have my own business, I have a good wife, good children, grandchildren. . . .
>
> "Yeah. He's still alive. Mostly we're quiet together. We eat, then I haveta get back."

Sam, age fifty-eight, was born in Eastern Europe:

> "My father? I never knew him. Killed in a pogrom when I was *seven years old*. My mother never got married again. . . . So, bu-

> behleh, what can I tell you about him? That he had a big red beard? That my mother saved his tallis for me—for nothing! I never wear it. That he left me with a family to support?
>
> "I tell you this. He was a big man, very strong—he smoked. I think I remember the cigar smell. . . . Yeah. He shtupped me with a strap. What else is a father supposed to do when a boy does wrong? . . ."

Perhaps, I thought, it may be that sons who are under thirty-five now, who denounce or criticize their fathers, are expressing a filial bitterness that may not mellow with time. Perhaps their grief and contempt are symptomatic or predictive of a new—and more bloody—ending to the psychopolitical struggle between fathers and sons.

Several men, in their late twenties and early thirties, told me of complete and contemptuous breaks with their fathers.

> "My father is a nonperson. How can I relate to a nonperson, who has literally nothing to say to me? . . . I am sorry, but not guilty, that he'll go to his grave without ever knowing who I am. He hates what he *thinks* I am—a rebel, a pervert. He doesn't love me. And I hate him."

> "My father tries to understand me. He gives me advice and money. He also refuses to understand that he can't understand. His liberal beliefs make me sick. He thinks he can reason with murderers. I think he's a sucker who can't help me, or himself, or the world he's so worried about."

More and more, as I listened, it seemed that many men had the same father. *All* the fathers began to merge into one man, one father-archetype: a shadow-stranger, part tyrant, part failed tyrant—pitied for the failure; an awkward man, uneasy or out of place at home; a tense man, not in control of his emotions; a man remembered for the blinding suddenness of his violence, for the blinding sweetness of his unexpected tenderness; a man of childish pettiness and of extraordinary generosity.

Sons, upon being asked, do try hard, in a rather unemotional, almost puzzled way, to remember these strangers, their fathers, for me.

Lawrence, a young man of about twenty-four, said this:

> "My father hit me a lot. But he had a lot to worry about, a lot on his mind. He was a champion wrestler when he was younger. . . . When I was about five, I remember, he hit me and I gave him an angry look and told him: 'Wait till I grow up. I'll be bigger than you and I'll beat you dead.' . . . My father was always sorry that he hit me but didn't know how to express himself. He'd never apologize, but he'd be very friendly, greet me loudly, when he came home, you know, unexpectedly. . . .
>
> "I guess he was depressed most of his life. He never had enough time, or he was always too tired to enjoy himself. . . . He liked 'big fun'—but he couldn't afford it.
>
> "He sits home and looks out the window now. Retired at sixty. He had to. But he's driving my mother crazy."

William, age sixty-four, born in rural Vermont, had more unhappy memories:

> "My family goes back to the *Mayflower*—but I'm sure there's an Indian princess in there somewhere. . . . We had land, a farm, enough food. But no money.
>
> "My father died when I was eight years old. What I remember about my father is very little—and very sad. When I was four, he and my grandfather took me out into the road and threw a huge ball—a baseball—at my head. I ran away to my mother, crying. I was the first son—after four girls—and I was scared of balls and of fighting. At least, at the beginning. . . . My father spanked me once or twice—when he should have.
>
> "Once a friend came to see him, kept complimenting him for finally having a son. My father got embarrassed, looked over at our hens, then down at me: 'If a rooster won't stand up for his hens, his head should be chopped off.' Gruesome thing for a father to say. . . . I was a complete failure at seven—as far as my father was concerned."

Even small boys can feel their father's emotional distance, suppressed violence or dis-ease. Steven, age eight, said:

> "He says I can't do anything because I don't know how.
>
> "Daddy has a loud voice. I'm scared when he yells. Daddy doesn't talk much when he's not yelling or making me do something like homework or clean up or go to bed.
>
> "Daddy is tired when he takes me and Laura out. He makes phone calls while we watch the movie. . . . I don't think Daddy has a good time at home. Daddies are like that."

What, then, is this father-son tension all about?

2. THE OEDIPAL DRAMA

The rage and (un)spoken accusations of fathers. The fears and (un)spoken guilt of sons. How easily we—and the social scientists—have forgotten that it was Laius, the father of Oedipus, who initiated the hostility by ordering his infant son killed, upon birth; and that it was Jocasta, the mother of Oedipus, who saved his life.

Florence Rush, in an unpublished study, found that American fathers resort more quickly than mothers do to *physical* or physically *violent* means of controlling or punishing a child—when the amount of time each parent spends alone with their children is equivalent.

There are only a handful of books and studies directly concerned with paternal hostility and violence toward male or female children. However, as with the subject of rape, I assume that soon there will be a proliferation of studies and books on this subject, including the shocking "hidden" prevalence of father-daughter incest, the sexual abuse of children at home, or commercially, in pornography or as prostitutes; the emotional terrorization and physical torture of children by their parents; and the intentional or unintentional murder of children by fathers and mothers.

Fortunately or unfortunately, it does seem that mothers tend to use verbal or psychological methods of child-control or -punishment. Partly this is because mothers think such methods are role-appropriate, and partly because mothers may think it does less "damage" than physical violence.

Mothers who *physically* abuse their children are often at the end of a long rope of time. Such behavior is quickly associated, in women, with extreme emotional and mental "disturbance"—and is treated accordingly when detected. Also it is worth noting that many detected cases of child abuse in fact involve mothers "taking the blame" and covering up for husbands and boyfriends—lest the act be more violently repeated, lest a needed source of income be lost.

The same child-abuse behavior in men is considered more "normal," in the sense that most men are assumed to have an intrinsically aggressive nature—one that is further encouraged by conditioning, one that is continually exacerbated by male-male competition outside the family sphere. Also, physically aggressive means of control or punishment are considered role-appropriate for men.

In reality, most fathers manage to minimize *physical* expressions of infanticidal or rivalrous urges toward sons. This is accomplished by placing small children into the enforced but protective custody of women. Infanticidal urges toward sons are also curbed by a psychological motive that overrides any feelings of rivalry: namely, men's need to combat death through reproduction. Sons represent their fathers' genetic re-creation, their father's longed-for lifeline to immortality. Paternal hostility is also minimized but never really resolved by what is often referred to as "the resolution of Oedipus."

It is often claimed that fathers want sons, but "prefer" daughters. Writer John Stoltenberg suggests that:

> Fathers fantasize all fetuses as male, as repositories of phallic life . . . he imagines that in a fetus, those lost, phallic feelings are contained and he can somehow have them back. If the baby is born without external genitalia, the father's projection of phallic life in the fetus stops. But if the baby is born a boy, the father's projection of phallic life in the infant continues.*

The so-called or hoped-for Oedipal resolution is far more concerned with fathers than with mothers: the Oedipal issue is not so much about a son's desire to possess his mother *sexually* as it is about a son's desire to avoid his father's hostility or disapproval in any way possible. Whether by "rejecting" identification with his mother, by identifying with his father, or by *not* identifying with his father, a son will choose whichever method achieves approval, safety, and a "safe" identity; whichever method staves off anxiety about any kind of castration.

Stoltenberg theorizes most plausibly about one major and basically "invisible" psychological event, among others, that prefigures or leads to the supposed Oedipal resolution:

> The boy will be a witness as the father abuses his wife—once or a hundred times, it only needs to happen once, and the boy will be filled with fear and helpless to intercede. Then the father will visit his anger upon the boy himself . . . [will punish him]—out of proportion to any infraction of rules the boy knew existed—once or a hundred times, it only needs to happen once, and the boy will wonder in agony why the mother did not prevent it. . . .

To escape the fate of the maternal figure, and to placate the father, sons then must decide something like this:

* John Stoltenberg, "Eroticism and Violence in the Father-Son Relationship," in Jon Snodgrass, ed., *For Men Against Sexism: A Book of Readings* (Albion, Calif.: Times Change Press, 1977).

> "I renounce my mother. I renounce *feeling* like her and being *treated* like her. I renounce my belief in her *power*. All this I do—in order that my father approve of me, in order that my father protect me from his own urges to kill or castrate me, in order that my father protect me from the violence of other men, in order that I *become* violent like other men."

This declaration of Oedipal resolution will never be enough to ensure total paternal love, or total filial rejection of or dis-identification with mothers. Psychologically, in fact, this ambitious voice of resolution continues its interior monologue forever—sometimes speaking aloud, sometimes remaining submerged in memory. But it is always visible in outward male action.

At least one other psychological event must occur—and it need occur only once, in order to ensure an Oedipal resolution. Specifically, the son must attempt to subdue or charm his father into a more compliant intimacy through a show of physical vulnerability or affectionate, physical closeness. This is what sons are probably used to doing with their mothers.*

However, such a show of vulnerability or affection by a son *cannot* work with a father. It is not *supposed* to. Women may be disarmed by a show of boyish, physical vulnerability or seductiveness—but most men are threatened by it. They see themselves in it and they know the consequences of such overtly erotic and "trusting" behavior toward another man. Fathers must teach their sons never to relate to other men in such a way.

Theoretically, a son need only approach his father *once* in such a way—and if he is rejected, if his show of vulnerability or seductiveness isn't effective, then this approach to another, more powerful man, can become permanently tabooed in a boy's mind.

Such an approach, and its failure, would partially explain how adult men relate to each other: with either undue defensive sub-

* Whether such an approach to either parent is "sexual," in an adult sense, is unclear. Certainly, it cannot be a consciously sexual approach, given how confused most five- or six-year-old children are about exclusively genital sexual activity.

missiveness or dominance. There is universal male relief upon being assigned either the "dominant" or the "subordinate" position in an all-male hierarchy—as long as the assigned rank is exactly clear.

Such repressed and forbidden sexual longing, together with *reactive* homicidal rage, leads to continual attempts at truce-making or "bonding" among men. ("Reactive" in the sense that fathers initiate the hostility and sons react either with hostility of their own, or, more likely, with guilt for having "provoked" the paternal hostility.)

Adult men fall into line behind a male leader in order to be spared the constant fear of not knowing when the next attack might occur. They fear having to withstand it alone. When adult men choose a male leader, they are assured of small but guaranteed portions of the spoils for themselves. Thus, "followers" are rescued from the possibility of no spoils at all, or from the possibility of greater insecurity, greater humiliation, or death.

Lower-ranking male members involved in group rapes are often "erotically" attracted to their leader. A boy's childhood display of vulnerability as a means of controlling or pleasing his father—and its failure—would partially explain this phenomenon. In fact, heterosexual gang-rape is a brutal and brutally clear expression of one major way in which the Oedipal dilemma is resolved. Fathers and sons make a pact based on a commitment to use what they share—a penis—on (or against) bodies-without-penises: female bodies. In gang-rape the mutual contempt for the "other" kind of body creates a truce—and within patriarchal marriage, the male "lawful" use of the female body represents another form of male-male bonding in normal "civilized" society.

Traditional, overt male homosexuality may be another effective resolution of the Oedipal dilemma. Many men do take this route in order to "bond" as strongly as possible with symbolic father or son figures. Yet this resolution is not socially sanctioned. Its repression or sublimation is what emerges as men's need for a sadomasochistic hierarchical order—whether among men or between men and women.

Male homosexuality may also be another way of attempting to minimize male-male violence, be it Father-violence or Son-violence. Male homosexuals, while they may fight over other men, over empires, over phallic destiny, will at least not be fighting among themselves over women. Traditionally, men have kept male-male violence to their notion of what is minimal through the exchange of women: a man gives another man his daughter for wife—and war, historically speaking, is less likely to happen between them. Women have also been used as ways of minimizing the potential violence between men.

Another "reason" for male homosexuality involves the hope of confronting, living out, or resolving the father-son relationship: a relationship which usually remains ambivalent, tragic, unresolved. Homosexuality is also a way of getting close to that member of your own sex who did *not* do the original parenting, and whose body you do not associate with infantile dependence.

Male homosexuality, like male heterosexuality, is also related to the patriarchal fear, hatred or envy of women as breeders. It is said that male homosexuals, artists, priests and warriors, are concerned with uniquely individual, transcendent contributions to existence. They are repulsed by the bloodiness of reproduction, by the predictable ordinariness of it, by their natural exclusion from it.*

Obedience to earthly and heavenly dictators is erotically fueled—by the renunciation of overt homosexuality. Paternal benevolence is passionately longed for, despite its obvious absence. So despite—or because of—life's tragedies, men insist that man's Father—God—exists, that He is good, *and* that He must be obeyed. This is the traditional male submission to the more dominant male.

* Men are not really "excluded" from the psychobiology of birth. In fact, most women feel they are presenting a miraculous gift to a *man,* not to themselves or to their mothers, when they bear "his" child.

This is one reason why it is so important for kings and contemporary political leaders to show or claim obedience to higher heavenly authority. The sight of a king, dictator, or oligarch kneeling before a male God, a male paternal authority, somehow obscures the inequality between male leaders and male followers. The ruler's obeisance before "higher authority" is meant to appease any chaos or insurrection born of humiliation and inequality among the ranks of male followers. Even the king, even the president, accepts the will, the authority, of a "higher" male figure. Thus are all men really equal.

The renunciation of overt homosexuality is also encouraged by the mutual sadism of men. What if, in expressing vulnerability and a desire to be protected and loved by another man, that (other) man turns out to be as distant or as dangerous as one's own father? Another man, a group of men, might abuse a homosexual man exactly as one's father did. The male homosexual is often treated as a devalued and feared woman.

Because it is so important to renounce the desire for overt homosexuality, men learn to express their real vulnerability and longings more safely: namely, privately, with a woman. She cannot easily refuse to satisfy male dependency, and a woman who is so dominated bears little resemblance to the forbidden and once-dominant Mother-figure. Thus, it is the renunciation of overt homosexuality which allows men to fuck, marry, and protect womb-men whom they also fear, despise, and envy. The renunciation of overt or total homosexuality ensures the propagation of the human race. . . .

To some extent, when men share "their" female property with other men, they are expressing their desire to satisfy forbidden homosexual longings in a socially approved and profitable way. Thus do fathers traditionally award or share their daughters with men of their choosing; thus do men often pay for political and economic favors or transactions between men—with women, i.e., with prostitutes; thus do an increasing number of men under forty in America, whether politically "right," "center," or "left," express "brotherhood" by sexually sharing wives, girlfriends or prostitutes. The dangerous urge toward brotherhood is more safely expressed through an unjealous exchange of (female) property: a commodity that men are used to fighting about. (Men feel very differently about "free love" when the women themselves initiate it, or do their own choosing—and are therefore no longer available as transferable "gifts" from one man to another man.)

Given the male dread and terror of other men, coupled with the male desire for paternal love, it is understandable that most men shy away from *vulnerable* and open-ended intimacy with each other. Rigid male rituals, such as handshakes or the ceremonies of fraternal orders, easily recognizable "signals" between men, are essential for male feelings of security. It is essential that men deny their unrequited love for, and their fear of, other men.

Sons transform their fear of fathers into a safer fear: a fear of or contempt for mothers. It is simpler for sons to remember an initial *physical* vulnerability toward fathers as a *sexual* vulnerability or temptation toward mothers, one which they have now (safely) renounced.

3. ON HAVING A PENIS

The difficult truce between sons and fathers proceeds from *both* recognizing the importance of what they have in common: a penis. This simple anatomical fact is what makes all men "like" each other and all men "different" from women. Based on this fact, men come to share a belief that women are not really human beings. This belief is so crucial and so deep that it remains psychologically "invisible" to both men and women. For a number of reasons, both men and women either deny having such a belief, minimize or confuse its importance, or claim to "prefer" its hidden advantages.

The consequences of this belief are enormous. By recognizing that *all* men possess penises, and by declaring that *this* is the root-sign of both humanity and true divinity, men may wince at the pain or humiliation inflicted upon other men, but not at the pain or humiliation inflicted upon women. This deification of penises allows men to *not* experience female suffering as representative of *human*—and therefore male—suffering. Female suffering is thereby condoned as less pertinent, less significant, less threatening than the pain which befalls men.

For example, most men are horrified at the forcible anal rape of another man. But they are much less horrified at the anal or vaginal rape of a woman, especially if she is not a female relative by blood or marriage. Also, most men experience any and all expressions of female emotion as overly intense and threatening, as a form of attack, as an attempt at female control. Women are often stunned by the rigid disapproval, the contempt, the *sadism* that men display upon being presented, within their own homes, with a display of female tears, or verbal demands and complaints.

Men behave this way because they are guilty: not for harboring patricidal wishes but for having betrayed their mothers, for having benefited, as a caste, from the emotional, economic, social, and political castration of women. Men sense that female "emotion" is dangerous because they believe at bottom it must include rage. But for a man to understand this and empathize with a woman accordingly is to admit to mother love; is to confess to psychological matricide; is to break the hard-won silence of father-son bonding. And psychically to betray and renounce patriarchal bonding is to invite male and female contempt, ridicule, and ostracism. According to John Stoltenberg:

> The son, in order to become as different from mother as he possibly can be, now begins to rid his body of the eroticism of the mother. . . . Every nerve in his body is on guard against her, against continuity with her, against the erotic continuum between them. . . . All the boy's sensibilities for erotic communion with other life become anesthetized in terror of ever again feeling one with the mother. The boy learns he has a penis and the mother does not. If he cannot feel his penis, he will be the same as her for sure. So begins the disembodiment of sensation in that small organ.
>
> Later in his life, the boy's eroticism will inhabit his penis exclusively, the part of him that is not mother. . . . He will discover to his frustration that the organ is anatomically incapable of sustaining

> that obsession. He will not be pleased after ejaculation, when the eroticism in his penis stops and when he feels a kind of deadness, the death of his phallic life. The more he has purged the memory of the mother from his body, the more and more his phallic eroticism must embody his whole sense of self. This is male identity, defined by the father, defined against the mother. This is male identity, in need of constant verification, in desperate struggle not to identify with the body and eroticism of the mother.

Most men are respectful of female suffering *in childbirth*—but do not identify with it. Men overdramatize childbirth pain or they cannot "face it"—or men "face it" by minimizing it. Or, as physicians, they frequently treat it sadistically. By comparison, women are both respectful of male suffering in all-male economic or military wars and *also* identify with it as a *human* hardship or tragedy.

It is *because* men believe that women, creatures-without-a-penis, are not human beings—that women are devils or angels, goddesses or whores—that many men *do* have a genuine urge to "protcct" women. They "protect" women, that is, from the consequences of being treated as extra- or superterrestrial beings. They "protect" women into corners where the harm they may do men is at least limited, minor, or limited to minors.

It is *because* men believe that women are not human beings that so many men are genuinely perplexed by, removed from, and cannot *identify* or empathize with female "complaints" of unhappiness, paralysis, disappointment, or anxiety.

Women, of course, have an equally difficult time really understanding male needs and are often contemptuous of the male need to be "taken care of" and "constantly agreed with." But women have been taught to value whatever men value and need—even when it hurts or confuses *them* as wives or as women. When wives develop close and independent female friendships, husbands are often unbearably threatened by the possibility of being gossiped about or ridiculed by creatures who do not share male biology. They also fear that their wives will "squander" maternal loyalty outside the family that is due to them alone, inside the family.

In a way, female one-to-one relationships function similarly to male "bondings": both are vehicles for enforcing conformity by containing, absorbing, and defusing the urge to nonconformity or socially dangerous thought or action. However, male group "bondings" serve additional purposes—and with different consequences.

Among men, the presence of a penis is still the proof of a shared and common humanity; still the proof of a truce between father and son, however uneasy a truce it is. It is still the trigger for male-male empathic identification.

Thus are adult men always comparing themselves to other men: on the basis of penis-size and physical strength. They always feel the need for male "truce," no matter the price. It is a transaction they have made once before. With their fathers.

Sons originally experience their "smallness" in terms of how small they—and their penises—are in relation to their fathers. The male idea or fear of being sexually castrated *must* involve some early fear of *fathers* doing this—as much as it may be "triggered" by contemplating the absence of a penis in the castrated mother, and in all women.

Remember: one interpretation of the Patriarch Abraham's willingness to sacrifice his son Isaac and the consequent substitute ritual of circumcision is that male gods and fathers can kill or castrate their young and even beloved sons, but can also choose not to. Sons, as they grow stronger, must gratefully remember having been "spared" and act accordingly, by "sparing" and by respecting their aging fathers.

Men, talking about "castration anxiety," seem to experience it, or associate it, with prolonged or intense heterosexual intimacy. Too intense or too "merged" a contact with women reminds men of their parent-without-a-penis who couldn't or wouldn't protect them from the parent-with-a-penis.

Men, upon being questioned about "castration anxiety," talk about their fear of vasectomies, about their fear of *any* kind of surgery or injury that would pierce or mutilate their bodies. All male blood that is shed is somehow experienced by men as a loss of sexual blood, as sexual mutilation. (Female blood, regularly shed, reminds men of their "castration" fear. It also reminds them of their deeply repressed desire to *bear* children, and of their inability to do so.) It seems as if male identity, or the *fragility* of male identity, actually resides in, or is best represented by, an exposed and vulnerable penis and testicles.

One twenty-five-year-old father of two children put it this way:

> "I've never been nervous about being castrated—not *really* castrated. I don't think about it at all. But I could never have a vasectomy. Never. It's not just that I couldn't have any more children or children with another woman. It's not that I'm afraid of losing my sexual desires or anything. It's a feeling I can't explain. It's a horrible, cold, numb kind of feeling—like what you'd feel about losing a leg in an accident, or having it amputated without anesthesia. . . . My wife tried to have natural childbirth and couldn't. I was with her, watching all the pain—I could never put myself through that. I imagine that's what it would be like—only worse."

Men, upon being questioned about "castration anxiety," either report having none—or immediately start telling me about how they fear being "castrated" by mothers and wives. They rarely mention fathers or other men. The silence of male truce runs deep; the fear of fathers is displaced onto mothers and surfaces in anecdotes about "castrating" women.

As I listen, I think: yes. Sons may have felt "torn in half" upon psychologically leaving and "denouncing" their mothers—but not in their *sexual* organs: in their entire bodies. Yes, sons probably do resent the female inability to rescue or protect them from their fathers, or from adult male competition. Sons may well resent being forced to "leave home" by their mothers—

who themselves can remain there, presumably safe from male violence.

Men, upon being asked about their penises (not about castration anxiety), often respond at first with a bristling, overwhelming concern with "size," with "quantities," and with "visible proofs" of penile activity. A thirty-one-year-old man said:

> "I can still have five erections in one session—especially with a new woman."

Many men responded to this question by telling me that "penis size isn't really important," but then told me how "lucky" they are to have a "good-size" penis.

When asked about having a penis, a fair number of men talked about "how many more orgasms a woman can have compared to a man." At least ten men referred to the "female use of vibrators," within five minutes of being asked about penises.

This particular pattern, of male focusing on female sexuality when asked about their own, this particularly aggressive insecurity, occurred repeatedly when I tried to talk to men about having a penis. It does seem related to male uterus-envy and, perhaps, to a newly awakened fear in men based on recent "discoveries" about female sexual capacities.

Absurd as it is, men tend to use male sexual behavior as the ethic, the referent, for human (sexual) behavior. Men assume that if women were as "free" as men, given the supposed sexual insatiability of women, they'd behave sexually like men, i.e., fearfully, promiscuously, as a means of identity-affirmation.

It is easy to understand why so many men are threatened, annoyed, disgusted, but almost childishly curious about recent research into female sexuality and orgasmic capacity. Suddenly to conceive of *women* entering the lists as sexual competitors—along with all other men, and with the natural advantage of a greater orgasmic capacity as well as a uterus—is both fascinating and repulsive to men. "Fascinating" because men are initially intrigued by anything that they can measure themselves against or compete against, to verify their own identity and existence. "Repulsive" because sexual competition between men *for* womb-men is one thing; but competition *between* men and womb-men—now that is too dangerous a reminder of buried womb-envy; that is simply too unjust, too pointless a competition to undertake.

"Sex," which for men always involves the presence of a penis, is crucial to most men as a means of identity-affirmation. And yet, men have retained an ancient—or a child's—terror of the power or "mystery" of female biology and sexuality. Men often describe or experience heterosexual forays as heroic rites of masculine passage: difficult, dreadful, triumphantly overcome, or quietly survived.

If men were not terrified of being found inadequate by the designated biological inferior; if men were not frightened and jealous of woman's reproductive capacity; if men were not disgusted by female sexual needs or demands—then female sexuality would not be so cruelly exiled into colonies of (sexually) undemanding girl-brides and girl-wives, or into colonies of (sexually) undemanding female prostitutes, concubines, or slaves.

Two writers, Renos Mandis and Andrea Dworkin, each explain the seeming paradox of male heterosexual sexual compulsivity despite male heterosexual sexual fear and loathing. In an unpublished article, Mandis notes:

> Don Juan is in perpetual motion. He cannot stop. If anything, masculinity is experienced as a "lack." It is something that you have to have which means that you don't "have" it. And you can "have" it only by doing it, in the sense that to know that you have it, you have to have an outward manifestation of it, an outside guarantee that you have to acquire again and again. In other words, it is only other people [who] can guarantee your masculinity. Or, you need this guarantee and feel you have to have it in order to survive.*

* Renos Mandis, "Don Juan Wants Kate Millett," unpublished article, 1974.

Andrea Dworkin concurs, in an exposition of male sexual compulsivity, and male devaluation or overvaluation of the heterosexual sexual act. She says:

> When men posit sex, violence and death as elemental erotic truths, they mean this—that sex, or fucking, is the act which enables them to experience their own reality, or identity, or masculinity most concretely; . . . and that death, or negation, or voidness, or contamination by the female is what they risk each time they penetrate into what they imagine to be the emptiness of the female hole. . . .
>
> What is experienced by the male as authentic (heterosexual) pleasure is the affirmation of his own identity as a male. Each time he survives the peril of entering the female void, his masculinity is reified. He has proven that he is not her and that he is like other hims.*

Since the penis is the proof of male existence, the proof of male power, it is too important and too vulnerable an organ to be exposed publicly—especially to women. While female nudity is everywhere exposed—in "great" art, in mass pornographic propaganda—male frontal nudity is relatively taboo. What if women began comparing the penises of aging husbands with those of younger, more "beautifully" shaped men? How could a man bear being compared, once again, by a woman, with *another,* "superior" man?

So it is no accident that recent paintings by women of male "frontal" nudes have aroused male (and some female) indignation, disgust—and wrath. I am referring to Sylvia Sleigh's paintings of male "frontal" nudes (see "Phallic Sexuality"). Often, community groups have demanded that her work be removed from museum exhibition walls. They have made no comparable protest about female "frontal" nudes in the very same show. In a recent book about sexuality in films, Joan Mellen, writing about Bertolucci's *Last Tango in Paris,* notes that:

* Andrea Dworkin, "The Root Cause," *Our Blood* (New York: Harper & Row, 1976).

> The imagery of the film is governed by the grand, machismo beauty of Paul and the inferiority of Jeanne: . . . She may be sexually vibrant and alluring, but she is without depth, real character or the capacity to rise to the role of heroine or rebel. Her entire body, complete with pubic hair, is continuously revealed to us because it is irrelevant to the dynamic of the film, as Bertolucci has admitted in his explanation of why he cut the shot he filmed of Brando's genitals. "I cut it out simply for structural reasons, to shorten the film," Bertolucci dissembled. Too honest, however, to allow himself this pretense, especially for a film so replete with the presence of the director, Bertolucci added, "it is also possible that I had so identified myself with Brando that I cut it out of shame for myself. To show him naked would have been like showing myself naked."*

But in sexual acts, a man's most private parts *are* exposed. How, then, do men feel about sex?

* Joan Mellen, *Women and Their Sexuality in the New Film* (New York: Dell, Laurel Books, 1973).

4. TALKING TO MEN ABOUT SEX

Men, upon being questioned about "sex," rarely accept as true anything that isn't true for them. Each man immediately relates any statement about male sexuality to himself, and accepts or rejects it, solely on the basis of his own experience. About "sex" men do not easily think beyond their own bodies.*

So—upon being questioned about "sex," men assume that what pleases them is, without question, exactly what pleases most other men, and certainly all women. To most men, to entertain the possibility of being "different" in sexual matters is to confront *the* basic attack on their normality, their masculinity, their humanity.

Despite professedly great interest in "sex," men traditionally have acquired very little genuine sexual knowledge—certainly almost no knowledge about what pleases other, female human beings. Men have been made to feel that they're *born* with all

* Although, as I've noted, men do, in a defensive and unconscious way, often project their own sexual feelings onto women—and then judge women harshly.

the sexual knowledge they need and that any attempt to improve on nature is already an admission of ignorance, failure, or weakness.

The sad fact is that most human beings have been conceived with only *one* parent having an orgasm. The fact is that most men have been fucking women who have *not* had, or known about, or thought they *should* have orgasms. And either men didn't know, didn't want to know, didn't care, or weren't capable of changing their own behavior so as to "combat" female sexual impotence. Perhaps it has always seemed enough to men that women could have babies and (presumably) be economically supported by men. Female sexual pleasure might be "going too far"; female sexual pleasure might lead to female sexual mobility—which would confuse the patriarchal laws of legal ownership of children. Female sexual pleasure is also "conduct unbecoming" a male-idealized concept of motherhood.*

Despite the male complaint about having to "perform," not too many men are overly willing to "perform" to please women sexually. Prostitution is important to men for many reasons—not the least of which is that they *don't* have to worry about female pleasure. They only have to pay money for their own. Of course, there are always a minority of men who *are* concerned with being able to satisfy women sexually: because they love them, because they themselves are "turned on" by it, or because they think that *this* is the major proof of male sexual prowess. But this is only a *minority* of men in the world—and a minority that is only recently vocal and visible.

When I ask men questions about "sex," they often warn me against overly trusting what other men have told me. "What

* Since men can't get pregnant and have totally repressed their desire to do so, it becomes important to men to be sure that their orgasm has produced a particular pregnancy: a very "visible proof" of penile potency, activity, and existence. Man's anguish about his own death is thus somewhat appeased by possessing and impregnating a womb-man in order to possess children, the products of his own sperm, the proof of his own orgasm.

have other men told you?'' they ask, each curious, each prepared to confirm or deny a stranger's statement, each ready to ''instruct'' me—if they can do so comfortably. One man said:

> ''It's not that men deliberately lie about sex. Exaggerating or agreeing with what other men say is how men talk to *men* about sex. Men might even be more honest with a woman than with a group of men about sex.''

Another man explained it this way:

> ''I don't think men are used to speaking honestly or freely about sex with *anyone*. Maybe what I mean is that I don't think that men mean the same thing by 'sex' that women do. . . . We might be talking about two different experiences and calling it by the same name.''

Some men, upon being questioned about ''sex,'' become rigid at the jawline, tense in their bodies, emphatic in their words, even more emphatic with their hands. As they speak about ''sex,'' these men's hands continuously, relentlessly, begin to drive home each point. It is so striking that after a while it seems to me they're showing me how they masturbate. A childhood of sexual frustration has been transformed into an erotic style that remains explosively and uncomprehendingly selfish, guilty, and defensive. Few men seem to have recovered from male childhood's enforced sexual distance from forbidden others—or from the shame and habit of secret, fantasy-driven masturbation.

When I asked men, ''Do you enjoy sex?'' the question seemed strange to them. Each man said ''yes'' very quickly. Then they explained themselves.

> ''Of course I enjoy *coming*. Who doesn't?''

> ''I guess I do. Why else would I fuck?''

> ''That's a peculiar question. All men enjoy sex. Maybe some women have hang-ups—but men? Fucking is as easy as jerking off.''

"Is it any different from masturbating?" I asked. One man answered:

> "It sure is. Especially if you can get her to suck you off. Or, if you really know how to appreciate a female body—the flesh contact makes coming much easier than when you're alone. Sometimes, you can get really turned on when a woman comes. You don't even have to imagine you're with someone else, or with two women instead of one . . . like I do when I masturbate."

Another man replied:

> "I feel the same *sensation* when I fuck and when I masturbate. Sometimes, it's better alone, and sometimes with someone else. Sometimes it's easier to jerk off than to go through a bunch of hassles and games when all you want to do is fuck. Sometimes the boredom or the big discussion of 'Do you love me?' takes away the pleasure. . . . When I jerk off, I can fall asleep right after, if I want to, without having a woman feel *abandoned*."

One thirty-eight-year-old man described a feeling of "heaviness" and of occasional panic after sexual intercourse with his wife.

> "She's all darkness, all sadness, all swollen need to me. I love her. I always return home. But I feel light, big, more *myself* with girlfriends—usually with very young girls, or with really independent girls, who don't expect to get married. Some young girls are really into *fucking*. It's all the meaningfulness they want."

Another man of forty described the same need to flee from a "loved" wife to more "voluptuous" women. His wife reminded him too much of himself, of his mother, and even of his daughter.

> "After you live with someone for fifteen years, you just aren't turned on anymore. I find myself thinking not of younger women—but of *older* women, of women my own age, the kind who in my neighborhood always *meant* sex. You know, dark and very open

> about it. . . . I guess I've always associated sex with non-Protestant and nonwhite women."

Many married men, upon being questioned about sex, reveal an almost universal preference for sexual intercourse in the morning. For men under forty, erections usually accompany waking. Men can acquit themselves quickly, jump up, wash, eat, and, already proven, escape into a day of all-male company: heroically away from the intimacy, the infancy of home.

Men of all ages talked about a preference for "quick" fucks: with prostitutes, with girlfriends, with male lovers—and with wives. Married men in small towns, who economically can't *afford* to pay for prostitutes, told me that they often arrive home at noon or at four o'clock to have a "quickie" before the kids come home, or while dinner is cooking. Or before it's time to go out with the boys. . . .

One wife in a small town said this:

> "He bothers me too much but what he wants is only a quick fuck. If I leave off cooking, or talking to my mother, he'll even help me with the dishes later on. It's worth it—giving in, I guess. Anyway I'm his wife. I don't really mind."

One husband told me this:

> "I hate my job; low pay, backbreaking work. The only thing that keeps my anger under control is fucking with my wife whenever I feel the pressure building up. Afterwards, I'm less tense, I can take one of the boys fishing, things don't seem so bad. Also, I drink a little less when she gives in to me."

The demand for speed, for "quickness" turns me cold. What demon do men run from? What enemy hovers behind them, what enemy waits to envelop them from within, if they pause a bit in the taking—if not in the giving—of sexual pleasure? Is this sexual style the inevitable conclusion of a childhood in which boys spend years trying to hide their erections, years of trying to masturbate in the dark—as quickly, as silently as they can, in order to avoid discovery? Is it such prolonged childhood silence that leads men into valuing loud noises, yelling out "dirty" words, or into a dependency on repetitious, visually exaggerated, closely detailed pornographic displays?

On being questioned about sex, one man told me:

> "Don't underestimate the importance of pornography, of pictures, of picture *objects,* in turning men on. You have no idea how much boys and men need magazines and films in order to jerk off, how much they think about it when they're fucking."

It is strange that men, who claim great—and greatly frustrated—sexual needs, should on the one hand demean their own sexual needs as "dirty" or as minor in importance and at the same time surround themselves with so many stimulants to "arousal." Male sexual images and the reality of prostitution both involve as little male sexual effort or energy as possible.

Men do not despise or minimize their other basic needs such as their need for food or oxygen. Men do not need other men to spur them on, to pressure them into breathing or eating, nor do they boast about doing these things, as they do about sex. . . .

I began to wonder about the meaning of a male sexual drive that needs so much arousal, so much help, so much understanding, in order that it be satisfied.

It slowly became clear that many men experience some postcoital disappointment, loneliness, a vague disgust, a sense of loss—and they encounter these feelings after sex often enough to wish that things were different, often enough to keep looking for a "change."

Men *have* lost something after intercourse: their sperm and their erection; and they have lost their sperm within a "foreign" body—within a body that is feared, despised, *different:* a woman's body. Or, they have lost it within another man's anus: a bodily part associated with excrement and taboo.

It is not surprising that so many men talk of a preference for being "sucked off." Being "sucked" means having less bodily contact with contaminated and tabooed body-parts; being "sucked" means less "work"—it most approximates the passive omnipotence of sexual fantasies; being "sucked" is often an expression of power over someone else—mainly because "sucking cock" is a culturally devalued act.

Despite patriarchal culture's basis in phallus-worship, most patriarchal religions have devalued "cock-sucking" as a nonreproductive, nonproductive act of pleasure. Like anal intercourse, "cock-sucking" is traditionally considered a one-sided expression of power.

Some men don't "suck" male or female others at all. However, the majority of men I talked with do—at least some of the time. Some admitted an initial queasiness. Many reported issuing instructions to women to "wash carefully because they smell bad." One man said that "vaginas *do* smell like fish or menstrual blood" but described his feelings this way:

> "I think it's only fair to reciprocate. I'll suck a woman if I really care about her, or if that's what she really wants. But don't expect me to carry on or pretend that I dig it more than I do. . . . I don't like it when a woman takes too long to come this way."

In heterosexual intercourse, men challenge psychic Death by risking what they feel is their most important and vulnerable organ—their penis—in order to experience transcendence, mastery, or self-definition. But all too often, afterward, men remain unchanged, unmoved, still mortal, and with nothing to *show* for what they've risked and lost. Afterward, men experience a "little death," or "petit mort."

One man told me that:

> "After sex I sometimes feel trapped or choked. I like to get up, walk around, smoke a cigarette, watch television. . . . I'm a little uneasy. Not depressed. More angry than sad."

Another man told me that:

> "I pass out after I come. My wife hates it but it's not in my control. This total kind of finish happens to me and I'm gone, passed out, like I'm dead."

Most men try to minimize the unique combination of postcoital sadness and disgust by paying as little attention as possible to these feelings—or they project the feeling outward, blaming a particular woman for *causing* the feeling, as if she, then, has become the repository of it and they, therefore, do not *intrinsically* have such feelings.

Men also minimize or repress this "petit mort" feeling in another way. Men compulsively search for ever-new, hopefully different female bodies, in the hope of escaping the domestic-vaginal home, the erotic maternal, the vagina dentata, the insatiable, the demanding, the transgressed-against and so guilt-inspiring mother-woman.

Men, upon being questioned about their enjoyment of sex, almost seem to be saying that what they enjoy *most* about sex with women is having it over with, especially when they feel they've acquitted themselves well. Acquitted themselves of any doubts about their virility or ability to "perform." Acquitted themselves of the sin or itch of lust: men no longer feel "horny" after they've come. Acquitted themselves of their need for a woman—for an inferior or dangerous being. Acquitted themselves of their religious and social obligations to procreate. Acquitted themselves of any charge of nonmasculinity that their fathers—or other competitive adult men—could accuse them of. . . .

5. PORNOGRAPHY AND OTHER MALE SEXUAL FANTASIES

If "masculinity" is something that must be acquired and demonstrated over and over again, in sexual as well as in other domains, in what ways do sexual fantasies enable men to succeed, sexually, in this venture?

Upon being asked about their sexual fantasies, many men describe pornographic scenes of disembodied, faceless, impersonal body parts: breasts, legs, vaginas, buttocks. Men of all ages fantasize, voyeuristically, scenes of whorehouses and male gang rapes; scenes of rape and mutilation; scenes of seduction and strangling; scenes of "clever" or omnipotent sexual control of extremely young and innocent children.

These are all typical sexual fantasies—found in magazines and films; these are the images that men masturbate to; these are the scenes that men try to act out in whorehouses; these are the images behind closed—or opened—male eyes, when they fuck.

It must be noted that most men (and women) do not fantasize the *actual* facts of an *actual* rape, but fantasize unrealistic and "idealized" rape scenes. The question remains as to what the connection is between such rape fantasies and rape as a real form of violence. It may be that actual rape is more easily minimized or misunderstood by those men who find idealized rape fantasies sexually "pleasurable."

The real-life consequences of pornographic fantasies, as well as their psychic meaning in fantasy, are very different for women and men. In one way, pornographic sexual fantasies function similarly for both sexes, by providing a temporary release from crippling sexual guilt, boredom, and culpability. Pornographic fantasies allow women freedom from guilt about their real or repressed masochism; and men, freedom from guilt about their real or repressed sadism. Otherwise, the fantasies function differently. In real life, women, not men, always risk a visible and devalued loss of virginity; a very "responsible" pregnancy; and a painful competition and rivalry with other women—for male attention, approval, passion, or love.

Pornographic sexual fantasies blur or soften female distress about male sadism, by allowing heterosexual women visual access to *other* women in fantasy, thus emphasizing and eroticizing the universality of the female condition. It also allows women the experience of sexual aggression by fantasy-identification with men.

It is difficult for most women to imagine or to be sexually aroused by imagining sadistic sexual aggression toward a *man,* or toward men. While lesbianism may be tabooed, female sexual aggression or sadism toward *men* is even more tabooed.* Most women, when they imagine "aggressing" at all sexually, do so against other women, in a male-like state of disassociation. This allows women to enjoy their own passivity, to avoid guilt feelings, and to engage in sexual aggressiveness and lesbian or bisexual desires—unconsciously and safely.

* Here, I am not talking about the men who pay prostitutes to whip or humiliate them. I am talking about what *women* want, and about the dominant sexual mores within the family.

Some men told me about "unique" sexual fantasies—at least they were fantasies previously unknown to me. Several heterosexual men had sexual "sports" fantasies. One man imagined that he was "up to bat, with the bases loaded, and when I hit a home run, I came." Another man was winning a yacht race; a third swore that imagining a football game—the smell of male sweat, the excitement of the crowd, the thrill of a touchdown—made him come faster or in a more exciting way.

Many heterosexual men reported some masochistic sexual fantasies involving either men or women, but apparently such fantasies are less common, less vivid, and less compulsively used than are sadistic fantasies. As based on my own experience and on talking to many women, it seems that few women of any sexual persuasion enjoy sadistic sexual fantasies with *men* as the masochistic objects. Only men do, usually homosexual men. Most heterosexual men cannot bear imagining themselves in the devalued female sexual role: at the mercy of other men.

Upon being questioned about their sexual fantasies, some men, like many women, insisted they had none—and definitely not during intercourse. But they insisted with such vehemence, such pride, that it seemed they thought it was more "manly" or more "normal" not to need the leftover images of childhood masturbation.

Ah. The male need to renounce and dis-identify with their mothers; the son's need to resolve sexual competition and other rivalries initiated by fathers; the inevitable fact of male sexual "aging"; and the long period of male masturbation in childhood. Looked at together, these needs and facts partially explain both the function and the pornographic or sadistic content of male sexual fantasies.

What can be considered a male version of menopause probably begins quite early—at age twenty-one or twenty-two. Its chief symptom, Don Juanism, or compulsive sexual "conquesting," is an attempt to return to, or to deny the loss of, male childhood and adolescent physiological sexual prowess, as well as to flee from heterosexual intimacy. Pornographic scenarios often feature older men, even "old" men, as ever-potent and forever capable of competing sexually with their own lost adolescent selves, or with their own sons. Fathers are extremely threatened by or ambivalent about the ease and constancy of their sons' or younger men's erections. Their rage is eased by pornographic sexual fantasies and by the realities they reflect, such as the continued access to many women or increasingly younger women that many men can expect, even though they age.

These same sexual fantasies also prepare impatient sons to "wait" their turn, since they are assured of having their "turn" for the rest of their lives. In this sense, such sexual fantasies are like legacies, inheritances, legal promises of acquisition. Paternal property, paternal ownership of women, *belongs* to sons, just because they have penises: if only they'll wait a little while longer, if only they'll do what their fathers expect of them.

Often, the sons of powerless fathers don't "wait" as long, since they are not promised a great inheritance, nor are they as clear about what is expected of them. The sons of powerless men are denied the emotion of father-respect, as well as the inheritance of property. Therefore their rebellion and their rage are not just against their fathers; it is also against father culture, which will not resolve things for them by settling something desirable on them in the future. The anger or sorrow of disinherited or powerless sons is analogous to what most economically poor people feel about being rich. Poor people are not usually against rich people, or against the meaning of being rich. They are only bitter about not being rich themselves.

Pornographic sexual fantasies also ward off the submerged, reactive, and rejected desire for heterosexual incest or intimacy. Few pornographic fantasies involve "older" women as the desirable sexual objects. By obeying the incest taboo—in reality as well as fantasy—boys are fleeing from their own (demeaned) infancy, dependence, and similarity to their mothers. Boys are also fleeing from what they've repressed: their father's jealousy or competition for maternal attention, a rivalry that ended in some kind of truce between men.

For such reasons, most pornographic fantasied sex objects are younger than oneself—not older. Only young boys and unruly male adolescents are genuinely and even romantically "turned on" by images of older women. It is a European and not an American tradition that favors both the sexual initiation of young men by older women and the taking of "older" women as lovers by men in their twenties and thirties. But when men begin to practice sexuality in reality, they usually practice on the easiest and most "attractive" women to get at: younger females, and females of obvious childbearing capacity.

Pornographic sexual fantasies serve two other major purposes. First, the image of pleasurably active or satisfied men—an image that whorehouses try to resurrect—helps men overcome or deny outright any feelings of passivity, fear, disgust, or inadequacy. Male physical fatigue or sexual awkwardness or mysteriously failing male sexual "interest" is denied in such "inspirational" sexual images. Rape fantasies—or sometimes real rape—reinforces men in the belief that they are superior to women and so can "have" a woman whenever they choose to.

Second, pornographic sexual fantasies are a major way of denying, absorbing, or *containing* male violence toward other men. Andrea Dworkin analyzes this phenomenon:

> The pornography of male sadism almost always contains an idealized, or unreal, view of male fellowship. . . . Each man, knowing his own deep-rooted impulse to savagery, can presuppose this same impulse in other men and seeks to protect himself from it. The rituals of male sexual sadism over and against the bodies of women are the means by which male aggression is *socialized* so that a man can associate with other men without the imminent danger of male aggression against his own person. . . . In other words,

> women absorb male aggression (sexually) so that men are safe from each other.*

In fantasy, then, no man has to be more "pleasing" than another man to merit sexual attention: no man has to be very sexually, economically, or socially powerful to *fantasize* that many kinds of women are at his disposal.

In *fact,* of course, economically richer and more powerful men *do* command more sexual attention, more easily and for a longer period of time, than economically poorer men do. But as long as the economically poorest of men has some sexual property and some illusion of male *sexual equality*—as long as men share the belief that every man is at least sexually (and therefore in every other way) superior to *all* women—the sharp and bitter edge of male rivalry is dulled, if not sweetened, by such shared patriarchal illusions—and by the opiate of pornographically induced male sexual orgasm.

Male emotions of rage, outrage, jealousy, and shame—toward more powerful men—are laid to rest, or acted out, in women's beds, or in pornographic sexual fantasies. Pacifying sexual orgasms help men avoid the even greater excesses—of fratricide or patricide—that would otherwise surely occur in the "dark Satanic mills" of male employment or on the male battlefields of war.

* Andrea Dworkin, "The Root Cause," *Our Blood.*

6. BROTHERHOOD

Upon being questioned about their brothers by blood, their male friendships and other male "bondings," men often stare at me, fall silent, accuse me of naivete—and laugh. Men tell me tales of being "knifed in the back" by other men; men remind me that all "top dogs" are deadly loners with no man for brother.

Men, upon being questioned about other men, use the phrase "top dog" or "chief ape" or "big gun" too often for me not to notice it. Do American men justify cruelty, or find it easier to live with, especially in the heartland of the myth of democracy, if they ascribe it to animal-based instincts in human beings?*

Oh, the stories of "top dogs" that middle-class men tell me! How they envy them, how they fear them, how they respect them!

* "Big guns": that's a weapon that no animal—not dogs, not even chimpanzees, with their slender-fashioned digging and poking tools—ever developed. "Big guns" have only been fashioned by the male human brain and hand.

The sly and clever "top dog," who fooled *even men* with passionate pronouncements of altruism, with fiery oratory about justice and "caring," until he got the only thing he "cared" about: money and some power.

The bold "top dog," who openly and steadily eliminated all male competition, with no mercy, with no personal animosity; a real machine of a man, a cool master of economic-class chess.

The "top dog" who inherited an empire, but who wanted men to *respect* him, not just to *like* him because of his unearned power—and so he developed a genius for recognizing false respect; an aversion to any real pity for him; a brooding allergy to the ambitious, "no-nonsense," very competent men who work for him, each of whom, in turn, he regularly replaces with someone "better."

The stories of "top dogs" that poor men tell me! The army officers whose very existence and function are to humiliate and physically abuse any recruit, any low-ranking man they don't happen to like, any man who is not sufficiently submissive.

Their memories of punishment: the solitary confinements, the extra duty, the "no passes home" are cruel and usual, are intimately related to the license later given them as soldiers to kill, to steal, to rape, and to commit cruel and usual acts of their own, during war.

Remembrances of "top dogs" among poor men are remembrances of practically everyone they've known. Teachers, doctors, policemen, judges, prison wardens, shop foremen, factory owners—all are remembered as "coolly" impersonal in their sadism, all as impersonally remembered as are the crime-chieftains and older gang-leaders in the neighborhoods of their childhood.

"Cool." As men talk about the "top dogs" in their lives, this adjective is an important, valued one. "Cool" denotes constant and knowledgeable activity safely disguised by corporate veils made of steel—or by poker-stiff faces; "cool" is used to describe sudden appearances, swift strikes, and equally sudden disappearances; "cool" as in cold; "cool" as in preserved forever, frozen; "cool" as in firm, unyielding, erect, and immortal. Everywhere, men judge and are judged by the language of penises.

When one listens to the answers men give to questions about "male-bonding," it becomes obvious that most men expect only competition and betrayal from other men. Most men do not turn to men for "brotherhood" or "sympathy." It is clear, as men talk about their relations with other men, with their blood-brothers, with their workmates, that men *are* in need of male sympathy. Which they don't often receive or trust when they do get it. And it is rarely given unconditionally, or selflessly.*

Men, upon being questioned about their real blood-brothers, remember their childhood fights and rivalries more easily than they remember any major fights with their fathers. In fact, a paralyzing bitterness is still heard in the voices of those adult men who are convinced that a brother was—or still is—their father's or their mother's "favorite" or "chosen beloved." Even when the parents involved are dead; even when the brothers have made "substitute" families; even when the brothers have come to "like" each other as adults.

"My problem," said one thirty-year-old man, "was being born first." "But," I said, "firstborn sons have an edge on attention and success. . . ." He interrupted me.

> "Yeah. But we have to do it strictly on our own. My younger brother—he's only *two years younger* than me—and my mother still calls him her 'baby.' She'd wipe his ass for him if he asked her. For him, she goes crying to my father for money. Me? She's lucky I don't need any help. . . .
>
> "I always got hit for starting the fights—even when I didn't. Her 'baby' was a liar. . . . Now, my brother comes to me with crazy business schemes, no cash, and my mother, she visits me with big

* That is why women are so important to men. We give "sympathy": but we are mothers, not fathers; we are the mother of God, not God, and not God's son(s). As I've noted earlier, in this regard, whatever women do is not quite enough for men who are love-starved for their *fathers'* sympathy.

eyes. She reminds me that we never got along, even as children, and 'isn't it time' for *me* to grow up and be a real brother? . . . Well, she has a point. But it's not fair. When is *he* gonna grow up and be an equal I can count on?''

One ''older'' brother, a man in his sixties, said he ''never talked'' to his younger brother. ''Why?'' I asked.

> ''Why would he want to talk to me? He's the success story in our family. Oh, we had an equal chance. I always failed. And he always succeeded. . . . He was more like my father than I was. He was a better hunter, more athletic, more of a man than me. . . . We just don't have anything in common. Well, maybe *I* don't think he's done everything strictly aboveboard, but in his position of power, that's hard to do.''

Another ''older'' brother, a man in his thirties, talked about his only brother, a younger, adopted brother.

> ''I don't know where that kid came from. I think from a military academy or something. He *loved* taking orders, kissing ass, dressing neat. . . . No, he actually believes in all that stuff about God and the flag. . . . I was the misfit. It's like *I* came from another family or from outer space. They (my family) always sat around as if they were really *happy* together.
>
> ''I think he did it just to spite me. And my parents are too dumb to see it. All they care about is being respected and what the neighbors think.''

''Younger'' brothers tell me of having followed their older brothers everywhere, only to be ordered back home, laughed at, or forced into doing whatever was needed—but considered ''beneath'' the dignity of older boys. From younger brothers, I heard stories characterized by either *extreme* fraternal protectiveness or *extreme* fraternal brutality.

One twenty-five-year-old middle-class man told me this:

> ''My next oldest brother got stuck with baby-sitting for me. My mother wanted him home, studying, and she also wanted him to have some 'responsibility' around the house. My father was never

there. My mother did a lot of charity work. So. He used to lock me in my room, go out, and swear to beat me up if I told my mother. I was six and he was twelve. . . . When I started having nightmares of the house burning down and I started to wet my bed—that's pretty poetic, don't you think?—my mother figured things out and I got a real baby-sitter."

Another "younger" brother, aged thirty-three, told me this:

"I have three older brothers. The only thing they ever got together on was hating me. They hit me to say 'hello.' I was the skinny kid. What could I do? I used to stutter. . . . Sometimes my eyes were black and blue for weeks. They used to do things that woulda killed my mother if she knew. In the beginning, they hit me to keep me quiet. Then, when I understood more, they didn't have to. I wouldn't say anything to hurt my mother.

"Lucky it never got to me. Knock on wood. But look at them. One bastard's in jail again, for armed robbery. They should keep him in there forever. The second one's crazy—really nuts. Maybe he always was. The one closest to me in age—he reformed. Took a regular job, got married, had a kid. We get together, we try to get along—but he still drinks too much. He talks too loud. My wife doesn't like him. So—we get together on holidays. For my mother's sake. What can you do?"

Male-bonding. Talking to most men about this subject is like talking to most women about male violence: you hear that it doesn't really exist—or at least that the men they know are "nicer" than other men. The men they work with are a "great" or an "okay" bunch of guys. Even when men *are* verbal about male violence, rarely do they piece together the tiny details into the larger picture of murderousness among men.

Men are used to thinking in "individual" and "personal-exceptional" terms: if the violence hasn't struck them, it doesn't really exist. Men are also used to thinking in "masculine" terms: they do not always see or are not always shocked by what men do to each other. To be male and label—or experience—too much male behavior as "violent" invites the disaster of discovering that one is different from other men.

Only Hollywood movies present male friendship as the mythic ideal—precisely because it doesn't exist in reality; because it is yearned for as ardently as men yearn for their fathers to love them, protect them, and name them heir to some legacy.

When men talk about male friendships or "bondings," their tone is matter-of-fact, unemotional, well-protected. They present themselves on "top" of the situation of unrequited fraternal love.

"Look," one fifty-year-old man told me, "the army is not like a Hollywood war movie." "But what about buddies?" I ask. "What about men saving each other's lives, mourning each other's deaths, going into business together after the war's over?"

> "Sounds to me like the movies convinced you. I fought in World War Two and in Korea. I had 'buddies,' but not like in summer camp for kids. Men in the army can't afford to become friends. Men can't afford to get too close to each other. You can't have a system of 'favorites' or 'best boyfriends' interfering with following orders or with performance. Your life depends on how well a stranger, a guy you may not like—and ditto—behaves. It can't have anything to do with whether you have 'personal' things in common. . . . You can't afford to be too upset when a 'friend' dies right next to you. How could you keep on fighting? If you got too depressed or confused, some *other* guy could die because of your mistakes. . . . *You* could die yourself. Men are 'buddies' with other men if they bleed red and know their job."

Another man, a forty-one-year-old politician, told me this:

> "Sure I got 'buddies.' Lots of 'buddies.' And we couldn't get too much done without coming through for each other. But they're not my friends. Can't afford friends when you want to get things done. Power isn't kept by a system of friendships. It's kept by how fast you can move with a change of time or need, how well organized

your people are, how easily you can drop another guy when he's wrong or going under . . . The people I *relax* with are in other areas. But even there, even with my wife's relatives, I gotta do favors, and I keep my ears open too. . . .

"I have allies and I have enemies, and I have my family. I have no *friends*."

One man in his mid-thirties described what happens each time two men meet:

"A lot of things go on. It's like two dogs circling each other and checking each other out. I mean you check out his economic scale. Is he manly? Is he tough? Is he great in sports? Is he okay? Can he help me? Can I help him? Is he gonna use me? Am I using him? Does he know a lot of pretty women? All these things take place in the course of a handshake. . . . Friendship could take place after some of these questions are resolved. After the competition is eliminated or channeled or accepted.

"It seems to me that generally when you first meet, men are vying to see who's going to have the top position. In most relationships you have with a man, there's always one who's on 'top' and one who's on the 'bottom.' Like an older and a younger brother. Like a father and a son."

Another man, in his forties, answered this way:

"I suspect that most men get together with other men, not because of the positives, but rather to compensate for a negative. In other words, guys hang out with guys because you're afraid that by being alone you may appear to be sexually inadequate, or you may have some other fear of inferiority. So you compensate for it. You hang out with the guys and you tell jokes, and you play pool and you act tough—or tougher, or you go along with some tougher guy . . . if you don't, whatever the action, you'll be excluded from it by the other guys."

A man in his early thirties responded with this:

"I have a feeling that a lot of men are so afraid of homosexuality that we do tremendous things to stave that possibility off. We *watch* each other to make sure we're all okay. Where I come from, to be a 'fag' is a low, terrible thing. It's the opposite of *everything* manly, everything good. . . . It's *not* like you may think. It's not the closest a man can come to being like a girl. You don't even think about a girl. It's far worse. . . . We run together, watching the next guy, hope he's watching us so none of us fall down on the job of keeping up. . . . I know this sounds crazy but I think it's what we do. I think it's one of the reasons men spend so much time together."

Upon being asked about male friendships, a man in his late twenties told me:

"You can become friends after a street fight, if nobody gets hurt too badly. It's acting out the competitiveness that a fight can mellow out. After a fight it's like two guys saying, 'I won't fuck with you and you won't fuck with me.' And each of us is free to fuck with anybody else . . . That's one of the ways that friendship can develop. You see, once you clear that air there, once you find out if the other man can fight, you can team up if it's a beneficial thing to do."

A man in his mid-thirties said this:

"I expect people will try to fuck over me. I think that's the way this life is. I become angry when people not only fuck over me, but try to get close to me—to really ram it in. That's what I don't like. It's like you see a guy who falls down on the ground and you say, 'Oh, that poor man. Let me go help him up.' And you grab him to help him up and he punches you in the mouth. Now you want to kill him. I should have kept walking like everybody else. That's what gets me mad—when I trust somebody.

"It's easier to have a relationship with a woman. Women aren't as competitive. They're warmer. They haven't been chopped up as much as men."

"Male-bonding": the containment of explosive and crippling male rivalries, the systematic containment of indiscriminate acts of male violence. "Male-bonding": the containment of the Oedipal dilemma, the containment of the urge toward male homosexuality—through the glorification of obedience to male "superiors," as heroes, or as benevolent father-figures with whom other men can identify.

"Male-bonding," in this sense, is not what women mean by friendship or by love. Male-bonding, in this sense, *is* an enviable "old boys' club" which is a system of controlling or sacrificing the majority of our planet's men and their female property for the survival, dominance, and comfort of a minority of men.

Many of the men I spoke to were well aware, at least verbally, of this sacrifice of the many for the benefit of the few. Yet, most men were more concerned with their own "winning," or with the *spectacle* of another man's "winning," than with eliminating, even rhetorically, the necessity for "winners" and "losers." In fact, most men seem to believe that patriarchal male-bonding is "natural," that is, that the role of the few male strong over the many male and female "weak" is rooted in primate and therefore human behavior, and that this state of affairs is a good one.

One man said:

> "We're living a finite life in a world that has finite and limited resources. These are tough truths that most people don't like to admit, but deep inside, they believe them anyway. There isn't enough of everything to go around and in any situation it's the best man or the best country who wins what it needs to survive at the highest level of culture."

I mentioned our century's high level of genocide, nuclear strike capacity, torture, totalitarian rule, terrorism, and the increase in poverty and planetary pollution. (To have included sexism and racism in my catalog of worldly sins would have "disqualified" me as a *serious* thinker.)

His answer:

> "The world's not perfect. I think that survival is better now for more people than ever before in history. . . . There have always

> been people who carry on about the world ending—but it never ended. I *still* think it'll go on long after you and I have bid it adieu."

The virility, the *manliness,* of such heartless realism. To accept, even embrace, all the suffering and destructiveness that exist, without guilt, without self-pity, without false hope—without compassion, for himself or others.

Such "tough" voices remind me of how fragile, how vulnerable I am rendered by my own instinct for justice. I am rendered childlike, innocent before statements such as this man's half-blind conclusion that "we live in the best of all possible worlds."

Like the man just quoted, most men do not easily complain about how things "are"—any more than they complain about their relationships with their fathers or with other men. Of course, male bonding presumably works to male advantage: perhaps there is less for men to complain about than I expect.

While there are countless examples of men destroying all male rivals completely, there are also many instances in which men "cover" for each other in vital ways.

How often have I observed middle-class men support another man of the same age through a painful divorce or a "mid-life" crisis, by inviting him to temporarily share the stability, the domesticity, the companionship of his own marital home, or by providing sexual or economic distractions for him. How often have I seen male judges and male juries pardon an accused man for crimes such as alcoholism, drug addiction, sexual "promiscuity," child abuse, child abandonment, for which women are never shown equivalent mercy.

And yet male-bonding is still basically an attempt to deny or at least to survive what really exists between men: men "bond" together only because (other) men are the deadliest killers of men on earth. Men "bond" only temporarily, to avoid, or to commit, savage acts of betrayal or humiliation of other men.

Male-bonding is about the lengths to which men are willing to go to gain male approval, or rather, to avoid male violence; male-bonding is about the male craving to inherit power from real or surrogate father-figures—power at least over women, if not over other men.

That men are dependent on women is clear—despite "manly" attempts to deny this; despite "manly" attempts to abstain from or devalue the dependency; despite "manly" attempts to punish women for being able to satisfy that which men need.

However, it is a mistake to confuse being depended upon or being "needed" with having objective power over him who needs you. Most women, as industrial or agricultural workers, as domestics, and as sexual mates, are relatively interchangeable and therefore relatively expendable on an *individual* basis. Also, the female fulfillment of male dependency fills men with a sense of terror, a sense of shame, a sense of having returned to infancy—and women must pay for that.

As I listen to men talk about male-bonding and male violence, I wonder to what degree male hostility toward feminist aspirations is related to a male fear of being abandoned by women—so that men would be left totally to themselves in an all-male society. Despite the male insistence on sex-separatism, most men need access to on-demand transfusions of emotional and physical relief or safety; to real or illusory—but on-demand and male-controlled—transfusions of intimacy, human warmth and "maternality": access to women, as fashioned by men.

Male-bonding is most conspicuously intertwined with fratricide and physical violence in the all-male society of jail. Where boys and men are confined together, with no access to women as displacement or absorption targets, their rage and shame are directed at other men.

MEN ON MALE VIOLENCE: THE VIEW FROM PRISON—I

PHYLLIS: I'd like you to tell me about violence in prison.

J.: I think the violence I saw was kind of a follow-up to schoolyard violence. It sounds funny, but the things that people committed violent acts over were generally very small things.

PHYLLIS: Give me an example.

J.: Okay. I witnessed several stabbings and a couple of murders. This, and serious fights, all took place because of either sexual things—fighting over a homosexual—or over gambling, over a few packs of cigarettes, an ego thing. You know, a guy would lose at some gambling game and say he wasn't going to pay and the other guy's ego got involved and it wasn't the debt itself but "My manhood's involved. . . ."

PHYLLIS: It's interesting that the first thing you told me about had to do with what goes on between prisoners. Supposedly the least powerful men there.

J.: Yeah. The guards—they're kind of a holding-action violence. I mean most of them recognize that they're in an outnumbered situation and they don't go out of their way. . . . I mean in the old prison movies you always have the sadistic guard kind of leering. . . . Sure, they would fuck over somebody, but they wouldn't go out of their way to do it. I mean it would be somebody who did something to them *first,* and got their ego involved.

PHYLLIS: What kind of "manhood" gets satisfied when it's a million to one?

J.: Well, it's that the whole majesty of their authority is being threatened—their uniform, their badge . . . because this is now a confrontation. . . .

PHYLLIS: What was the most brutal thing that was done to you in prison?

J.: Well, I guess the thing that I thought was the most brutal was how they got me there. Personally speaking, I think the most violent things that were done to me were done by the courts and the police. Not so much in beating me but in the way I was arrested. This particular charge was a railroad, you know.

PHYLLIS: By whom?

J.: A person I had formerly been in jail with and who I thought was a good friend of mine.

PHYLLIS: What was the effect on you emotionally to discover that you had been set up? By a friend?

J.: Well, originally my first response was, I just wanted to kill myself. That was my first impulse. But then after I thought about it, the second response was to get him, you know, this guy. And I really did try. I mean, frankly, when I got out on bail I asked where I could get a gun. That was my move . . . but I couldn't find him . . . he was supposedly a friend of mine—it was really a horrendous thing. About two years later, he killed himself. He took an overdose of drugs. I read about it in jail. I really got angry and I said, "That mother-fucker. How could he do that to me?" Because, like my first response was, he was taking away my— I was going to do that.

PHYLLIS: Do you think you would have killed him?

J.: What I really wanted to do was maim him. You know, punish him—but badly, put him in a hospital. Really do a number on him. And I felt that if he then tried to find me or get back at me, then I would kill him. . . .

MEN ON MALE VIOLENCE: THE VIEW FROM PRISON—II

LESTER: Jail is synonymous for violence. Almost everybody in jail has been humiliated through the state. I mean, *no matter what they did.* And they, in turn, humiliate each other.

For example, take a new man who comes into the prison. . . . Somebody will attempt to "hit" on him. . . . Now this inmate has a choice. He can either say, "You know, I'm not gonna do it''—or he can do it. There may be some attempt at force, but if he really resists, it won't happen. The inmates don't want to get into a hassle with the authorities. Also, the new dude might fight back and someone might get hurt.

PHYLLIS: Does the first ''hit'' usually take place on a one-to-one basis?

LESTER: No, it's usually a gang rip-off.

PHYLLIS: A gang rip-off?

LESTER: Like one dude will be trying out somebody. He'll hit on him just conversationally, see what cues he picks up. And then another dude follows. Then, if they decide that this is a person they can rip off, it will be maybe three or four who will rip him off in his cell.

PHYLLIS: How can one guy defend himself against three or four guys?

LESTER: Well, maybe he can't at that instant, but the cues were presented beforehand and he could have stopped it then with the right responses. Once, a kid got ripped off in his cell by four guys and he was in pain, bleeding very badly. They took him to the hospital. . . .

PHYLLIS: Didn't anyone have any mercy or pity for him?

LESTER: Very little. The person who gets raped is not considered a victim but a mark. He's the one who's shunned. He gets segregated for his own protection for a while. Then, when they let him back in population, everybody will fuck with him.

PHYLLIS: Did anyone ever beat you up or rip you off in prison?

LESTER: No. But I'm, you know, pretty big. And the cues come off. I can be beaten—but generally guys would look at me and say: ''Why fuck with this guy?''

PHYLLIS: You're a loner-type . . .

LESTER: Yeah, well I don't need to be close to anybody.

MEN ON MALE VIOLENCE: TEENAGERS IN CONFINEMENT

PHYLLIS: Tell me about the boys you work with.

BARRY: I'm a counselor in a home for delinquent boys. They're kids under eighteen who've done everything from kill, torture, and steal—to play hooky, wet their beds, or sell their bodies to older men for quarters. . . . No one knows what to do with them. They're right out of *Clockwork Orange,* but they're *kids*.

In the beginning, I tried to accept them and get them to accept me. There were four counselors for every fifteen boys in a dormitory. They were *manageable*. But this changed when they built bigger dormitories. Then, there were twenty-five boys in each room. And fewer counselors.

All of a sudden, if a kid throws a fork in your face it's witnessed by twenty-four other boys. All of a sudden, the counselors get paranoid—which means we get tough. Now, when one boy "expresses" himself, it can lead to a group riot.

One kid throws that fork, and unless you make him regret the day he ever went for it, then fifty kids see it and accept it as *possible*. The level of acceptable violence graduates pretty quickly.

What happens when the newspaper boy walks in and all of a sudden ten bored, frustrated guys decide to take it out on him? One guy gets up and pushes the newspaper boy, and another guy goes up, and all of a sudden, you see ten individual identities becoming almost like a universal group identity. They lose themselves so much that they'll stomp the kid right to death, if they're not stopped. Something wild, cold, driven comes over them. They're not feeling anything. They're just acting out somebody else's orders. The Devil's maybe. They can't stop it. What's weird is they don't always look like they're enjoying themselves. They're *here* but they're not here.

I'm not so threatened. Who *is* threatened is anyone who can't take the strongest guy on—physically.

Here's an example: A boy comes back. He's the type of kid who says "yessir" all the time—and rips down buildings the minute you're out of sight. This kid is thirteen years old. He's used to raping the younger kids. He's used to "I can make someone turn over in bed for me. I'm stronger than he is." But we've managed to eliminate sex play while he's been away. We encouraged the younger kids to tell us what happened by rewarding them and punishing the kids who made them do it.

Anyway, this kid is in the infirmary after two days back. And he tells an eight-year-old: "I want to take your buns." That's the phrase for it. The thirteen-year-old is 140 pounds—much heavier than the eight-year-old.

They fight. The smaller kid gets two teeth knocked out but he makes enough noise to attract some adult attention. Now, what am I gonna do with this kid? He's coming back to our dorm after attempting to rape an eight-year-old!

Now, I told him: "Listen. Any trouble from you and I'm gonna see you go to Senior Side and you're gonna have guys sixteen and seventeen years old over there . . . and they're gonna throw you around like an eight-year-old."

"Man, okay, I don't wanna get raped," he says.

He's a leader type. He'll form a gang on the outside. A "youth gang," and get them to swagger around the neighborhood together. Fighting, extorting, dealing, raping: maybe they'll beat up on drunks. . . . If he lives, he'll try to get into something bigger. He'll try to deal himself into some bigger action with men from out of the neighborhood.

And thus do father-abandoned or father-wounded sons become "fathers" themselves: killers of other men; great Godfathers and petty tyrants; terrified of intimacy, consumed with an unredeemable fear of other men.

EPILOGUE

In parting, dear Readers, should I weave a word-spell for you to sleep by for another ten thousand years? A faery tale perhaps: all about an enchanted Princess, an evil dragon, a great treasure, a brave young Prince, and how they are once more safely stitched up into a tapestried procession of bakers and tailors, doves and chariots, jugglers and jesters, mares and steeples, and the inevitable Great Ladies and Gentlemen come from afar to join the sunrise in celebrating the marriage of Two Kingdoms. . . .

Ah, but this favorite bedtime story no longer holds enough magic. For example: there are more uninvited wedding guests in the story than ever before. No more does One menacing figure sit alone waiting at the Gate; no longer does One have to come in disguise. Here, look, you can see them: marching in medaled uniforms. To a man, they are all much older than the Prince— who has not conquered Them in Himself—and so there can be no happy ending.

There is another reason that tempers my temptation to tell you a faery tale. It is this: that we are not children and need more than faery tales to comfort or save us. All of us, set adrift in the twentieth century, are irretrievably grown up. All of us born after 1918; certainly all of us born after 1933; and especially those of us born after the explosions of 1945—we are born old, knowing too much about Death.

Our genes, if not our conscious minds, know that something is awry; our genes know that we are an endangered species arrived too soon at the Gates of 1984, propelled there by "progress"—an overgrown, unchecked progress!—that allows more men to systematically or reactively maim, torture, and kill more people, more scientifically, than ever before in History. Sanity and Survival are the Twin Princesses who lie asleep inside the castle of History, surrounded by this very same rose-encrusted, progressive overgrowth.

Never have we needed a Hero more than now: when our usual human greed and cowardice are so coupled with the possibility of fatal, final accidents. Never have we needed a miracle more—now that we know there are no miracles; now that we know that it is peace, not war, that "breaks out," and then only occasionally, in film, not in fact, and never Forever After.

A hero. A hero who is not put out to die at his Father's command. A hero who does not abandon his Mother. A hero who does not become his own Father, or an impersonal or dictatorial "Father" to other men. A hero who is not killed by his brothers and then worshiped afterward. A hero such as we've never known: in whose name youth is not cannibalized and broken; a hero in whose name war is never declared, countries are never colonized, people are never enslaved, and women are never raped; a hero in whose time poverty, illiteracy, loneliness and conformity are unheard-of. . . . Now this, my friends, is the true Faery Tale: simple, serious, thoroughly uncharming, not the stuff that rapid industrialization, preventive deterrence and smiling, unlikely trade delegations are made of.

Dear Readers: I must admit something to you. Yes: I save news clippings. I paste them up in journal-notebooks and flatten them down into labeled file-folders. And why, you may ask? Because they cradle the past and predict the future: more brazenly than any store-front fortune-teller, more seductively than any Masked Lady at a circus. News clippings are the fine-grained lines crisscrossing the hand of Time. I read them over and over again, looking for clues, for memories, for confirmation.

They, my collection of news clippings, my record of "recent" events, are the real reason I will not tell you a made-up faery tale. I blame them, my record of bloody deeds in black-and-white, for my sense of urgency, and for my sense of future happenings.

I know: newspapers rarely tell us about "good" things. "News" is about accidents, tragedies, disasters, far worse than our own, to help resign us to whatever our fate may be; to allow us, vicariously, to congratulate ourselves at the greater misfortune of others. But newspapers don't lie completely. The information they barrage us with does, increasingly, challenge our imaginative humanity and our collective responsibility.

So I have been reading the tale of History as the most important Faery Tale of them all. I used to believe what I was told: that nothing ever changes. But lo! In reading the papers, I began to see that here, in this clipping, is a turn of the spiral usually hidden from view; and here, in this other clipping, is a turn of the screw: positively new!

Dear Readers: Long before I wrote this book about Men, I "unconsciously" chose certain events of His-story from newspapers. Now, when I look at all the clippings again, I see the terrifying battle between Fathers and Sons—which most Sons have always lost—confirmed; I see how every day Eve is punished again for man's anguish over Paradise Lost—and for her childbearing abilities.

In terms of "brothers," I see that Cain kills Abel, Joseph is sold, the Jews enslaved or sent into exile, and Christ killed—at least once a week. Corporate firms pollute their brothers' earth, air and oceans. For pride, for profit, scientists lie to their brothers about cures for disease—while they build spaceships for the escape of the wealthy to new planets. Then, only then, will the poor truly inherit the burnt-out earth.

The plunder of Beirut, the total destruction of Vietnam: what a terrifying future—and ancient—face of civil chaos, greed, and what the Fathers now call "limited warfare." The dangerous increase in "illegal," or Son-terrorism, is surpassed by the more dangerous increase in "legal," systematic, or Father-terrorism.

What I write about in this book has been "illustrated," actualized, in the following tales, told by New York City newspapers, and by a handful of other news publications. Imagine the picture if I'd pieced together excerpts from a thousand papers!

FATHERS KILLING SONS

BOY, 3, IS BEATEN TO DEATH IN BRONX; FATHER IS ARRESTED

A three-year-old boy was beaten to death last night, and his 28-year-old father was arrested and charged with murder.

The father is also under investigation for the beating of his older son, 4-year-old Eric, who was listed in serious condition at Fordham Hospital last night with a broken left arm and right foot and bruises about the body, and burned feet.

New York Times, Feb. 13, 1973

BLIND BOY, 13, SAYS DAD SLEW SISTER AND BROTHER

JACKSONVILLE, Fla. (AP)—A 13-year-old boy who police say was blinded by his father has testified his father killed two other children and stuffed their bodies into plastic garbage bags.

Young Ernest testified that his father had tortured him and the other children by choking them, jabbing fingers in their eyes, beating them on the feet with a broomstick and slamming their heads on the floor.

"He put me under the water in

the bathtub and hit me a lot. He choked me and kicked me I don't know how many times. He broke my arm but I don't know how because I fell unconscious in the bathroom trying to hold on," the boy said.

New York Post, March 28, 1974

SLAYS BOY IN SACRIFICE TO INDIAN GOD

NEW DELHI (AP)—Police in Uttar Pradesh State have reported that a merchant has confessed killing a 12-year-old beggar boy in expectation of becoming a millionaire.

Police in the town of Lar, 200 miles southeast of New Delhi, said the merchant had severed the boy's head on a July festival day devoted to Shiva, god of destruction, after fattening him up for a week.

A Sadhu (holy man) told the merchant he would become a millionaire if he satisfied the god with a human sacrifice, police reported.

A month ago in Rajasthan a similar ritual murder of a 12-year-old boy was reported and four people were arrested. They are awaiting trial.

New York Post, September 12, 1968

VIOLENCE AND BRUISING LABOR PLAGUE CUTTERS OF PULPWOOD

The man stood at the rear of a pulpwood truck operating the winch. Sweat dripped from his face.

His 19-year-old son Bob hooked the tongs into a thick five-foot log that appeared to weigh several hundred pounds. Another son, 13-year-old Luther, who is small for his age, sat behind the steering wheel and revved the motor to power the winch.

The father yelled. The boy cranked the engine again, the winch groaned and then a third time, in spite of Luther's efforts, the engine died.

The father ran to the cab and hurled the boy to the ground. He began slapping the boy's head and face with his open hands. Then his fury increased and he struck him several times with his fists. Finally, he snatched a pine bush and lashed the boy on the buttocks until the strength left his arms and his curses died and the boy stopped crying aloud. . . .

New York Times, June 30, 1974

3 U.S. PILOTS ARE PUNISHED; ERROR IN BOMBING KILLED 105

Saigon, April 12 (AP)—The U.S. Air Force has reprimanded

three of its pilots, docked their pay and temporarily grounded them for the worst bombing mistake of the Vietnam War.

The strike killed 105 Montagnards (mountain tribesmen) and wounded 250 in the village of Lang Vei, in the northwest corner of South Vietnam.

This was the first report of disciplinary action taken against U.S. personnel responsible for a bombing mistake in the Vietnam War. About a dozen such incidents have been reported, with about 500 casualties.

Both the two-seater F4C Phantoms dropped anti-personnel cluster bombs which missed the camp and fell into the nearby village.

New York Post, April 12, 1968

SONS KILLINGS FATHERS

I.B.M. EXECUTIVE IS KILLED IN UPSTATE HOME; SON HELD

VESTAL, N.Y., Sept. 16 (UPI)—Norman Madsen, Sr., an executive of I.B.M. World Trade, was stabbed to death in his home in this Binghamton suburb last night, the police said. His son, Norman Jr., 20 years old, was later arrested and charged with first-degree manslaughter.

The police said that Mr. Madsen, 47, and his son apparently had argued during the night. . . . Mr. Madsen reportedly had been stabbed in the back.

New York Times, September 17, 1973

BOY WHO KILLED PARENTS AND HIMSELF LED SECRET LIFE OF TORMENT AND DOUBT

Four days before Gregg Sanders, a 15-year-old boy from Mountainside, N.J., killed his parents with an ax and then threw himself to his death from a water tower, he was reprimanded by his history teacher. He was worried about it.

Gregg took up a two-foot ax and killed his father with several blows to the head and then killed his mother the same way.

Perhaps the most revealing discovery was the existence of Gregg's secret room. . . .

A two-foot-high wooden panel,

apparently made by Gregg, had a large swastika on it with the inscription "Amerikanische Nazi Partei." There were armbands with swastikas and a six-page handwritten manuscript of quotations from Adolf Hitler.

New York Times, February 3, 1975

SONS PRACTICING

GANG MUTILATES AND KILLS BRONX MAN

A South Bronx man died yesterday several hours after he was set upon near his home by a gang of a dozen youths who beat and sexually mutilated him.

Detectives identified the victim as William Battles, 31 years old . . . and said he was wearing women's clothes when he was attacked.

Detectives said several witnesses believed the attackers, who ranged in age between 14 and 20 years, were members of a youth gang.

New York Times, November 25, 1973

STRANGLING OF BOY, 3, IN BROOKLYN IS 3rd RECENT CHILD MURDER HERE

The strangling on Monday of a 3-year-old Brooklyn boy, allegedly by a 14-year-old mentally disturbed youth, was the third child murder reported here recently.

In another death of a child, two teen-aged boys were held yesterday in connection with the rape and murder of a 9-year-old Bronx girl thrown to her death from the 20th floor of a building. . . .

She was taken at knifepoint to the roof where . . . she was forced to perform various sexual acts and then pushed to her death.

New York Times, June 27, 1973

GIRL, 10, STABBED TO DEATH "FOR $10 BET"

"It was a bet. She died because someone bet someone else that he didn't have the guts to do it. Someone took a dare." So said a Vancouver detective today explaining why 10-year-old Kelly McClain . . . was stabbed 47 times with a sharp target knife in the bathtub.

Because someone took seriously a $10 bet with two young

friends—a bet made in jest, the friends later said—the girl was stabbed over and over after hiding under a blanket in the belief she was just playing hide-and-seek. After the last thrust of the knife, a suspect, allegedly a 16-year-old boy, picked up the phone and called the police.

"We found nothing, nothing to warn anyone that he would be a violent person."

Vancouver Sun, August 24, 1976

TORNADOES RIP CHICAGO; RAMPAGING YOUTHS KILL WOMAN IN STALLED CAR

Tornadoes slammed into a Chicago suburb last night, killing two persons and injuring 23. Torrential rains hit the city, and youth gangs roamed the South Side, attacking stranded motorists. Police said one gang had killed a woman in her stalled car, and at least 15 other persons were assaulted.

Phyllis Anderson, 51, was shot to death and her husband Leo, 51, critically wounded when they refused to pay a gang $10 to push their car across a flooded bridge. . . .

Police said that in another attack, Edward Rosen, 35 . . . suffered a broken jaw and wounds to the left cheek when attacked by youths carrying baseball bats. . . .

New York Post, June 14, 1976

BROTHERS

HOLD TWIN IN STABBING OF BROTHER

Police have charged a Bronx man with stabbing and slashing his twin brother to death in the rundown tenement apartment the two shared.

Police said that Byron Frowner, 39, slashed his brother repeatedly in the limbs and chest with two eight-inch kitchen knives during a protracted struggle last night. . . .

New York Post, November 24, 1976

FIRMS HID DATA ON CANCER

WASHINGTON—For at least a year, chemical firms in the U.S. and Europe withheld significant scientific findings linking liver cancer to a gas used to make one of the commonest plastics. . . . The trade association of the American chemical industry, the Manufacturing Chemists Assn., joined in holding the findings in confidence.

New York Post, May 22, 1974

HAZING RITE "BURIAL" KILLS JERSEY STUDENT

N.J., Nov. 12—William Flowers, a 19-year-old Monmouth College student, suffocated early today when a sandy "grave" he was forced to dig in the rainswept beach as part of a fraternity initiation collapsed as he was lying in it.

The victim of the hazing incident was reported to have been the first black allowed to pledge for the fraternity.

New York Times, November 13, 1974

ARKANSAS PRISON REFORMER MAY BE MADE THE SCAPEGOAT

CUMMINS PRISON FARM, Ark.—Thomas O. Murton, the prison superintendent who unearthed three skeletons in what he believes is a cemetery for slain convicts, is in danger of becoming the scapegoat of the bizarre affair.

It was difficult to determine whether the legislators were more outraged at Murton's public announcement of the finding of the graves or the fact that persons whose cause of death was uncertain occupied the crude wooden coffins.

"What are we going to prove by all this sensationalism?" Rockefeller asked.

New York Post, February 6, 1968

ST. JOHN'S STUDENT KILLED IN HAZING

A 20-year-old Queens student was stabbed to death last night during a moonlit military hazing ceremony conducted by an ROTC fraternity on a tiny island in Great South Bay.

Edward Fitzgerald [the victim] was "captured" and a wooden plaque reading "prisoner of war" was hung around his neck.

Savino was assigned to play a Russian officer, whose job it was to interrogate Fitzgerald to obtain "classified information."

Apparently, Savino . . . used a 10-inch military knife to threaten Fitzgerald and kept stabbing at the plaque around the pledge's neck. On the last thrust the knife plunged into Fitzgerald's chest.

New York Post, November 6, 1976

SALVADOR RIGHTIST GROUP THREATENS TO KILL JESUITS UNLESS THEY LEAVE NATION

SAN SALVADOR, July 17 (AP)—Right-wing terrorists have threatened to kill 50 Jesuits unless they leave El Salvador. The Jesuits say they will stay to help the nation's peasants fight what they charge is exploitation.

In a statement accusing the priests of "Communist subversion," the right-wing White Warriors Union threatened to kill all members of the Jesuit order in this Central American country if they did not leave by Thursday.

"The executions will be immediate and systematic," said the clandestinely distributed statement from the group, reportedly made up of retired army officers linked with government security forces. . . .

El Salvador's military government has ruled almost uninterruptedly since 1932. It is controlled by a few families that own 60 percent of the land in this country of 4.5 million people, 90 percent of them Roman Catholics.

Church sources said that after the Jesuits became involved in the peasant struggle, 15 priests were expelled, five denied re-entry, two slain and eight tortured by the police. Most of the victims were Jesuits.

New York Times, July 18, 1977

RAPE OF BEIRUT RECALLS THE PLUNDER OF PARIS

BEIRUT—Not since Adolf Hitler and Hermann Goering systematically looted Paris during World War II have the spoils of a city at war been so thoroughly gleaned as those of Beirut.

The rape of Beirut has been so massive that it may be years before its extent is fully known, according to bankers, businessmen and black market sources here. But they estimate the total at $1 billion.

The looting is estimated to have exceeded $300 million in the port of Beirut alone.

About two-thirds of the material, according to reliable sources, was taken by the rightists to finance arms purchases and personal fortunes. The remainder went to the leftist-Palestinian side. Both factions included free-lance looters who raided the port strictly for their own benefit, said a black marketeer.

At one British bank, according to a witness, two Christian factions, the Chamounists and the Falangists, simultaneously hit upon a vault literally filled with cash and negotiable travelers checks, held there for clearance from other banks in the Middle East. After a brief fire fight—in which six men were killed—to establish proprietary rights to the treasure, the two "allies" made a truce and blew the vault with high explosives. The Falangists took $6 million in cash, and the Chamounists $12 million in travelers checks, which later cleared in Switzerland.

Most of the readily marketable goods, such as expensive appliances and TV sets, have already been exported—overland to Syria, Jordan and the Persian Gulf States, or by sea to Greece and Cyprus.

Truckloads of refrigerators, stoves and other kitchen appliances have been seen winding along the Beirut-Damascus highway, en route to Syria. It is not certain whether Syrian troops, who make up virtually the entire peacekeeping force here, are involved in the smuggling. But it is inconceivable that the convoys have been moving without their knowledge.

Some of the smaller-scale looters, described by a black market source as "The guys with real guts," used the downtown hotels of Beirut as if they were department store showrooms before shells destroyed the buildings completely.

New York Post, 1976

SONS KILLING MOTHERS

WOMAN SLAIN—SON HELD

NYC—An ailing 76-year-old woman was found beaten and strangled in her Washington Heights apartment early today after police say her 46-year-old son telephoned to "911" to announce he had killed her.

Neighbors . . . said the son had exhibited odd behavior since returning from [Bellevue], but his mother had assured them: "He's my son. He won't hurt me."

New York Post, 1975

SON IS HELD IN MURDER OF MOTHER

NYC—A 25-year-old Queens man was in custody today after allegedly killing his mother in their Woodside apartment while a crippled and mute younger brother struggled to get help.

She was found lying head down in a bathtub of bloody water.

New York Post, December 30, 1974

EX-CONVICT GIVES DETAILS OF SEVEN WEST SIDE MURDERS

Calvin Jackson, the 26-year-old former convict who is said to have implicated himself in the murders of 11 women on the West Side, has provided authorities details of seven killings that could have been known only by the slayer, investigators said yesterday.

Mr. Jackson . . . has been charged formally with one murder, the alleged strangulation of Mrs. Pauline Spanierman, a 69-

year-old widow, in her apartment. . . . [Jackson] implicated himself in at least a total of 10 homicides—Mabel Martmeyer, 60; Blanche Vincent, 71; and Eleanor Platt, 64, . . . Winifred Miller, 47, . . . Kate Lewisohn, 65, who was found dead of a skull fracture on July 19, 1973, and Yetta Yeshnefsky, who was found dead of stab wounds on April 29, 1974.

New York Times, September 15, 1974

2 YOUTHS TELL OF KILLING MOTHER AND DAUGHTER, 9

FREDERICK, Md. (AP)—Police found the bodies of the victims—the mother and younger half-sister of one of the two suspects—where the two men told them they would. "[The murderers, aged 18 and 20], weren't upset. They were both laughing about it," Police Chief Charles V. Main said.

"They didn't have a motive, just said they didn't like them. It was strangulation by clothesline."

New York Post, April 16, 1974

HELD IN KILLING OF WOMAN, 66

A 24-year-old former mental patient was charged today with stabbing to death a 66-year-old woman who lived down the hall from him in a West Side welfare hotel.

"She was like a mother to him, she fed him, she sometimes even gave him money," said Mrs. Jean Sands, 62, who also lives on the floor. "He ran errands for her; she used to send him to the store. I can't understand it."

New York Post, October 11, 1974

BOY TELLS OF ROLE IN KILLING OF HIS SISTERS

DETROIT(AP)—A Detroit [14-year-old] teenager has told a Criminal Court Judge he participated in a rape attempt with three other youths that led to the knife slayings June 30 of his 11-year-old twin sisters.

New York Post, August 22, 1968

MANACLES AGAIN FOR L.I. KILLER?

DeNicola, who has said he killed on orders of the Devil, erupted in court as a defense psychiatrist traced his motives to his younger sister. The shackles were placed on him at his own request because he feared that "I will kill someone if I have to listen to that stuff about my sister."

"She was pure, perfect, and God-like to him," Dr. Brian P. Lipton of 67 Park Ave. was telling the jury of 11 men and one woman.

But just before the wedding, DeNicola was disillusioned. He

had learned that his sister was pregnant. . . . "That devastated him," said the psychiatrist. "He was enraged at his sister for her sexuality, loss of control and loss of virginity . . ." "Nine days after his sister's marriage on what must have been an overwhelming impulse," said Dr. Lipton, "he murdered another Patricia [Sullivan] as a symbolic representation of his defiled sister and his female self . . ."

New York Post, April 24, 1974

CANDLELIGHT PRAYER, TORTURE AND DEATH IN A SWISS CHALET

Zurich, Switzerland, May 20 (AP)—They used to sit together in their little chalet, praying by candlelight to the Virgin of Fatima for peace in the world.

To increase the force of their prayer, they drank champagne.

And in between prayers, they whipped the daughter of their former president, 17-year-old Bernadette Hasler, who died last weekend after a month of systematic torture.

They confessed to police they beat her "to drive the devil out of her."

Among the arrested are Bernadette's parents, farmer Josef Theodor Hasler, 41, and his wife, Leni, 39.

Police said Hasler told them he wanted to cure his daughter of sexual urges. He gave her into the care of "Father" Josef Stocker, 60, head of the sect, also under arrest.

Police said Stocker, a German, was a Roman Catholic priest who was excommunicated for fraud several years ago. Stocker and his German mistress, Maria Magdalena Kohler, 52, conducted most of the prayers and the beatings of Bernadette.

Members of the sect claimed Bernadette had "a dirty mind."

To cleanse it, police said, they tied her to her couch and beat her regularly. Three to five persons used to take part in the whippings, police said.

New York Post, May 21, 1967

ARAB "HONOR" & WOMEN'S LIVES

BEIRUT(CDN)—Women who bring "dishonor" to their families are murdered by their brothers or other male relatives at an alarming rate even in the most sophisticated of Arab cities.

. . . [One] young man decapitated an unchaste sister and carried her head to the authorities as proof that he had restored his family's honor.

. . . [A] study revealed that murders of women by male relatives, because of real or suspected adultery, prostitution or premarital sex account for more than six per cent of all homicide convictions in Beirut and just under eight per cent of those in all of Lebanon.

New York Post, March 22, 1974

WOMB-LESS MEN

EX-SUITOR STILL LOVES THE GIRL HE SUED TO PREVENT ABORTION

An unemployed construction worker who obtained a temporary court order barring his former girl friend from an abortion says he's still in love with her.

It bars Wendy Chasalow, 19, from having the abortion before the full Supreme Court hears her ex-boyfriend's arguments Monday. She had planned to have it yesterday.

"I care for her and she could be hurt by this," he said. "I'm not doing this just for me. It's for her. She has a lot to lose—a family to lose, a college education. She has just me to gain."

New York Post, April 22, 1977

SPERM DONOR WANTS TO VISIT BABY: MOM OBJECTS

BRIDGETON, N.J.—A judge has been asked to rule whether a sperm donor can visit the child he fathered through artificial insemination—despite the mother's objections.

Court papers said the mother did not want to marry or have sex, but wanted a child of her own.

New York Post, April 22, 1977

CHARGE PORTER IN KILLING OF WIFE IN FAMILY COURT

A 35-year-old Transit Authority porter was charged with murder today after he allegedly stabbed his wife to death in Family Court, as they waited for a hearing to decide who would get custody of their son.

New York Post, November 30, 1976

HACKED BODY—MANY CLUES BUT IT'S STILL A MYSTERY

FERNRIDGE, Pa. (AP)—The case is full of clues—a body

chopped into 10 pieces, a fetus, three suitcases and soggy pages from the Sept. 26 New York Daily News.

The remnants of the body and the fetus were packed into the suitcases, then hurled from a 300-foot-high bridge. . . .

The woman was in her late teens or early 20s, had brown hair, brown eyes, was 5′4″ and weighed 150 pounds. The fetus was a near full-term female. . . .

New York Post, January 7, 1977

SPERM SEPARATION: "FILTERING OUT" FEMALE BABIES

Several dozen very special babies are about to be born around the world, and up to 90 per cent of them are expected to be males because of a Sausalito man's new idea.

Dr. Ronald Ericsson, a reproductive physiologist, claims his method, in research the last five years and confirmed by five independent studies, "offers the best that people have to offer."

The babies will be born in Asia, Europe and in North America (specifically, California and Illinois).

Population Reference Bureau, a major nonprofit educational organization, said today that the Ericsson method "could have major implications for population planning, particularly in those countries where a strong preference for male children prevails."

"The technique," it added, "holds no promise for parents of sons who long for a baby daughter."

The bureau conceded that this patented idea could be viewed as tampering with nature.

Ericsson insisted that no tampering was involved. "We're offering the best that people have to offer."

San Francisco Examiner, September 28, 1976

ANNOTATED BIBLIOGRAPHY

Aeschylus. *Agamemnon.* Translated by E. D. A. Morshead. In *Seven Famous Greek Plays.* New York: Random House, 1938, 1950.

Bakan, David. *Slaughter of the Innocents: A Study of the Battered Child Phenomenon.* Boston: Beacon Press, 1971.

Bakan quotes Darwin as noting that civilization began with the "onset of infanticide." In this brief volume about child murder and abuse, Bakan suggests infanticide and cannibalism as the hidden themes of the Garden of Eden myth. Bakan also analyzes children's fairy tales as ways in which children signify their recognition of paternal ambivalence and hostility toward them. I obviously agree with him.

Baldwin, James. *Nobody Knows My Name.* New York: Dell Books, 1961.

A writer's autobiography of one American black man's experience.

Balswick, Jack O. "Attitudes of Lower-Class Males Toward Taking a Male Birth Control Pill." *The Family Coordinator,* April 1972.

Balswick notes that "perhaps these men feel that tampering with their own reproductive system or sexuality is more a violation of nature or of their sexuality than it would be for the female . . . The most common objection to vasectomy was 'I don't want to be cut on'

. . . 'I don't want no doctor foolin' around with me' . . . to the lower-class male (black and white), the fathering of children is often thought to be a sign of masculinity . . . while any tampering with his reproductive potential may be defined as emasculating." Where are the studies of middle- and upper-class men? Are *their* attitudes not well represented here?

Barker-Benfield, G. J. *The Horrors of the Half-Known Life: Male Attitudes Toward Women and Sexuality in Nineteenth Century America.* New York: Harper & Row, 1976.
A remarkable, historical study of the origins of patriarchal obstetrics and gynecology and the nature of sexual repression and misogynistic surgical savagery in America.

Bart, Pauline. "Portnoy's Mother's Complaint." *Women in Sexist Society: Studies in Power and Powerlessness.* New York: Basic Books, 1971.

Beels, C. Christian. "Whatever Happened to Father?" *The New York Times Magazine,* August 1974.

Bellow, Saul. *The Adventures of Augie March.* New York: Fawcett Publications, Crest Reprint, 1949.
A writer's autobiography-fiction of one man's Jewish-male experience.

Bergler, Edmund. "The Clinical Importance of 'Rumpelstiltskin' As Anti-Male Manifesto." *American Imago* 18 (1961).

Beukenkamp, Cornelius. "Phantom Patricide." *Archives of General Psychiatry* 3 (1960).
Read this for the tone of sexism and mother-blame so typical of psychiatric journals.

Biller, Henry R., and Borstelmann. "Masculine Development: An Integrative Review." *Merrill-Palmer Quarterly* (1968).
Read this paper primarily for its bibliography.

Boyle, Margaret Taylor. "Bibliographic Review of the Literature on Incest." Unpublished bibliography, 1975.

Broner, E. M. *Her Mothers.* New York: Holt, Rinehart & Winston, 1975.
Broner has some superb portraits of men as fathers and as lovers, and of women as mothers and as daughters.

Brontë, Emily. *Wuthering Heights.* New York: New American Library, Signet Classic, 1958.

Brown, Norman O. *Life Against Death: The Psychoanalytical Meaning of History.* Middletown, Conn.: Weslyan University Press, 1959.

Brownmiller, Susan. *Against Our Will: Men, Women and Rape.* New York: Simon and Schuster, 1975.

Bugliosi, Vincent, with Curt Gentry. *Helter Skelter.* New York: Bantam, 1975.
An excellent account of the Charles Manson Family's murders and trial.

Campbell, Joseph. *Hero With a Thousand Faces.* New York: The World Publishing Co., 1949.

———. *The Masks of God: Occidental Mythology.* New York: Viking Press, 1964.

———. *The Masks of God: Creative Mythology.* New York: Viking Press, 1968.

Castaneda, Carlos. *Journey to Ixtlan: The Lessons of Don Juan.* New York: Simon and Schuster, 1972.

Conroy, Frank. *Stop-Time.* New York: Dell, 1965.
Autobiography of one American-Protestant male experience.

Dansky, Steven. "A Night Song for Rose, My Mother." *Double-F: a magazine of effeminism,* no. 3 (Winter, 1975–76).

Dostoyevsky, Fyodor Mikhail. *The Brothers Karamazov.* 2 vols. Translated by David Magarshack. Middlesex, England: Penguin Books, 1958.

Dumezil, Georges. *The Destiny of the Warrior.* Translated by Alf Hiltebeite. Chicago: University of Chicago Press, 1969.

———. *From Myth to Fiction.* Translated by Derek Coltman. Chicago and London: University of Chicago, Press, 1970.

Dworkin, Andrea. *Our Blood: Prophecies and Discourses on Sexual Politics.* New York: Harper & Row, 1976.

Exley, William. *A Fan's Notes.* New York: Random House, 1974.
A stunning autobiographical novel of a very literary male in America: the fully grown male as perpetual adolescent, rendered holy and touching even in his sexism, even in his divine obsession with barstools and football games.

Fanon, Frantz. *The Wretched of the Earth.* Translated by Constance Farrington. New York: Grove Press, 1963.

———. *The Wretched of the Earth.* Translated by Hackon Chevalier. New York: Grove Press, 1965.

Farrell, Warren. *The Liberated Man: Beyond Masculinity.* New York: Random House, 1974.

Feigen Fasteau, Marc. *The Male Machine.* New York: McGraw-Hill, 1974.

Ferracuti, Franco. "Incest Between Father and Daughter." *Sessuologia,* 1967. Translated by G. McLaughlin. Report No. 21, Office of the Prison Psychologist, England, 1968.

Firdausi. *The Shahnamah.* In Yohannan, John D., *A Treasury of Asian Literature.* New York: New American Library, 1959.
The medieval Persian epic of a father killing a son in battle—mistakenly or "unconsciously."

Fradkin, Howard E. "Incest." *Family Practice News,* January 1975.
In *Women and Madness,* I wrote about the dominant psychosexual model for women as being that of rape-incest-and-procreation. Only recently has father-daughter incest been admitted to be a widespread and highly destructive act.

Frazer, Sir James George. *The Golden Bough: A Study in Magic and Religion.* New York: The Macmillan Co., 1958.

Freud, Sigmund. *The Basic Writings of Sigmund Freud.* Translated and edited by Dr. A. A. Brill. New York: Modern Library, 1938.

———. *Moses and Monotheism.* Translated by Katherine Jones. New York: Random House, Vintage Books, 1939.

———. *Civilization and Its Discontents.* Translated by James Strachey. New York: W. W. Norton, 1961.

Fromm, Erich. "The Oedipus Complex." *The Crisis of Psychoanalysis.* Greenwich, Conn.: Fawcett Publications, 1970.

———. *The Anatomy of Human Destructiveness.* New York: Holt, Rinehart & Winston, 1973.

Gager, Nancy, and Schurr, Cathleen. *Rape: One Every Two Minutes.* New York: Grossett & Dunlap, 1976.

Gil, David. *Violence Against Children.* Cambridge, Mass.: Harvard University Press, 1970.

Goncharov, Ivan. *Oblomov.* Translated by Ann Dunnigan. New York: New American Library, Signet Classic, 1963.

Green, Richard. *Sexual Identity Conflict in Children and Adults.* New York: Basic Books, 1974.

Helfer, R. E., and Kempe, C. H. *The Battered Child.* Chicago: University of Chicago Press, 1968.

Henden, Herbert. "Black Suicide." *Archives of General Psychiatry* 21 (October 1969).

Henley, Nancy. "On Sexism and Racism." Published as part of the report of the Sub-Committee on Women of the Committee on Equal Opportunity in Psychology, February 1971.

Herrmann, Kenneth J., Jr. *I Hope My Daddy Dies, Mister.* Philadelphia: Dorrance, 1975.

This short, anecdotal book by one child-protection-agency worker describes a week in his work life. Mothers physically abandon, abuse, torture, and maltreat their children—and while his contempt for them is great, his belief in their own despair and ability to change is equally great. This same tone of contempt and expectation is not used to describe what fathers do: as if somehow, paternal abuse is an irreversible form of deviance. He describes police reluctance to allow him to "remove a six-year-old child whose father had punched him repeatedly and had smashed the boy's head on the concrete stairs leading to his home." He describes a father who forces all five of his daughters to have sex with him—and beats them until they do. Since three daughters are too frightened to testify the court can do nothing, except place the daughter who complained in a foster home. He describes a scene of terror in which the father of ten children, who just "comes and goes," returns, drunk, demanding the money from a welfare check. When he cannot find any money, he "punched [his wife] in the mouth. At that, Jimmy [the six-year-old] ran at him. His father threw the boy to the floor and kicked him in the face. He then grabbed the next closest child, the seven-year-old, by her arm, picked her up and threw her into a chair. . . . Jimmy was admitted [to the hospital] with broken teeth, a broken nose, and facial bruises." The father was never found. Herrmann describes a middle-class father losing his temper and beating up his four-year-old son, kicking him in the stomach, and fleeing the scene "when Billy refused to come into the house." The mother describes the father as "basically good, but he needs help. He didn't mean to do this, but he can't always control himself." Another father killed his six-month-old son by throwing him down the stairs about one in the morning. "The baby was crying, wouldn't stop, and . . . the father went into a rage."

Holy Bible, King James Version.

Horney, Karen. *Feminine Psychology.* New York: W. W. Norton, New York, 1967.

Hough, Robert. "The Male Mythology of War Ecstasy in a Gynandrous-Androgynous Universe." Unpublished article, 1974.

Janeway, Elizabeth. "The Weak Are the Second Sex." *Atlantic Monthly,* December 1973.

Janis, Irving L. "Groupthink." *Psychology Today,* November 1971.
Read this for thoughts about male conformism.

Jung, C. G. "Four Archetypes: Mother, Rebirth, Spirit, Trickster." *Collected Works,* Vol. 9, part 1. Translated by R. F. C. Hull. Bollingen Series. Princeton, N.J.: Princeton University Press, 1959, 1969. It is interesting that Jung notes that "a woman can identify directly with the Earth Mother, but a man cannot (except in psychotic cases) . . . the (normal) man identifies with her son-lover."

———. *The Freud/Jung Letters*. Translated by Ralph Manheim and R. F. C. Hull, and edited by William McGuire. Bollingen Series. Princeton, N.J.: Princeton University Press, 1974.

18 December 1912

Dear Professor Freud,

May I say a few words to you in earnest? I admit the ambivalence of my feelings toward you, but am inclined to take an honest and straight-forward view of the situation. If you doubt my word, so much the worse for you. I would, however, point out that your technique of treating your pupils like patients is a *blunder*. In that way you produce either slavish sons or impudent puppies (Adler-Stekel and the whole insolent gang now throwing their weight about in Vienna). I am objective enough to see through your little trick. You go around sniffing out all the symptomatic actions in your vicinity, thus reducing everyone to the level of sons and daughters who blushingly admit the existence of their faults. Meanwhile you remain on top as the father, sitting pretty. For sheer obsequiousness nobody dares to pluck the prophet by the beard and inquire for once what you would say to a patient with a tendency to analyze the analyst instead of himself. You would certainly ask him: "Who's got the neurosis?"

. . . If ever you should rid yourself entirely of your complexes and stop playing the father to your sons, and instead of aiming continually at their weak spots took a good look at your own for a change, then I will mend my ways and at one stroke uproot the vice of being in two minds about you. . . . I shall continue to stand by you publicly while maintaining my own views, but privately shall start telling you in my letters what I really think of you. I consider this procedure only decent.

No doubt you will be outraged by this peculiar token of friendship, but it may do you good all the same . . .

Most sincerely yours, Jung

3 January 1913

Dear Professor Freud,

Although you have evidently taken my first secret letter very much to heart or very much amiss, I cannot refrain, while avoiding that topic, from offering you my friendly wishes for the New Year. . . .

Don't hesitate to tell me if you want no more of my secret letters. I too can get along without them. . . . So if I offer you the unvarnished truth it is meant for your good, even though it may hurt.

I think my honorable intentions are perfectly clear, so I need say no more. The rest is up to you . . .

Most sincerely yours, Jung

6 January 1913

Dear Professor Freud,

I accede to your wish that we abandon our personal relations, for I never thrust my friendship on anyone. You yourself are the best judge of what this moment means to you. "The rest is silence" . . .

Yours sincerely, Jung

Kafka, Franz. *Letter to His Father.* New York, Schocken Books, 1974.
A remarkable, painful exposure of self—and of his father.

Kazantzakis, Nikos. *The Greek Passion.* New York, Simon and Schuster, 1953.

Kierkegaard, Søren. *Fear and Trembling and the Sickness Unto Death.* Princeton, N.J.: Princeton University Press, 1954.

Knoebel, John. "Toward the Unmaking of a Catholic Priest." *Double-F: a magazine of effeminism,* no. 3 (Winter, 1975–76).

Knox, William, E., and Kupferer, Harriet J. "A Discontinuity in the Socialization of Males in the United States." *Merrill-Palmer Quarterly* (1971).
The authors note that "the objects, processes, and the symbols of the male youth's cultural experiences in the U.S. today ill equip him for his adult family roles. Close to the root lies a deep belief, imparted early and overgeneralized, that feminine traits and behavior in the male connote emasculation."

Koestler, Arthur. *The Case of the Midwife Toad.* New York: Random House, 1971.
Read this for a story of male-male competition and cruelty among "civilized" men.

Krim, Seymour. *You and Me.* New York: Holt, Rinehart & Winston, 1968.

Lear, Martha Weinman. "Is There a Male Menopause?" *The New York Times Magazine,* January 1973.

Lederer, Wolfgang. *The Fear of Women.* New York: Harcourt Brace Jovanovich, A Harvest Book, 1968.

Legman, Gershon. *Rationale of the Dirty Joke. An Analysis of Sexual Humour.* New York: Grove Press, 1968.

Lerman, Rhoda. *Call Me Ishtar.* New York: Doubleday, 1973.

Lerman retells fairy tales and myths brilliantly, but read her, especially, for a literary-theatrical depiction of full, female sexuality, involving sacred rites and young(er) men—depictions very far from our culture.

I am indebted to Lerman for her verbal description of the Goddess aspect of the Torah, which she shared on a panel in Detroit, Michigan, June 1976.

Malinowski, Bronislaw. *The Father in Primitive Psychology.* New York: W. W. Norton, 1927.

Mandis, Renos, "Don Juan Wants Kate Millett, or Men in Trouble." Unpublished article, 1973.

Mann, Thomas. *Joseph and His Brothers.* Translated by H. T. Lowe-Porter. New York: Alfred A. Knopf, 1974.

An enormous literary accomplishment, a long symphony: meditative, passionate, timeless, and, certainly, All About Men—and their brothers.

Marin, Peter. *In a Man's Time.* New York: Simon and Schuster, 1974.

Male autobiography, California.

Mead, Margaret. *Male and Female: A Study of the Sexes in a Changing World.* New York: Morrow & Co., Morrow Paperback Editions, 1975.

Menninger, Karl. *Man Against Himself.* New York: Harcourt, Brace and World, 1938.

———. *The Crime of Punishment.* New York: The Viking Press, 1966.

Milgram, Stanley. *Obedience to Authority: An Experimental View.* New York: Harper & Row, 1969.

Read this for a view of male conformism, obedience, in hierarchal form, in the following of orders.

Miller, Jean B. "Sexual Inequality: Men's Dilemma. A Note on the Oedipus Complex, Paranoia, and other Psychological Concepts." *American Journal of Psychoanalysis* 32 (1972).

Miller notes that when men become paranoid, "they often talk about persecution by other men . . . when women become paranoid, they, too, tend to talk about assault by men, not by other women . . . 'Normal' men dream about men twice as often as they dream about women. Women do not dream correspondingly about women . . . If aggression occurs, the attacking figure is most often a male in both men's and women's dreams . . . Those with whom men are seeking full communion and confirmation become the people who are most threatening and the most to be feared. Men in general seem constantly to be seeking to be valued in the eyes of other men and to be simultaneously on a keen alert to the danger that one slightest weakness may put them at the mercy of other men."

Moloney, James Clark. "The Psychosomatic Aspects of Myths." *American Imago* 18 (1969).

Myers, Steven A. "The Child Slayer." *Archives of General Psychiatry* 17 (August 1967).
This study reviews 83 child murders committed in Detroit between 1940 and 1965. It notes that 30 "mothers" killed 35 children and were nearly all judged "insane" and treated accordingly; and that 41 "people" (no sex given), including 10 "fathers," killed 48 children, and were as likely to be sent to prison as to a mental asylum. Myers notes that "manual assault was generally committed by the victim's father or by a young man left in charge of the victim. These assaults were frequently in response to a sudden, intense, uncontrollable rage, experienced by the assailant after the child had defecated on the floor or could not be quieted from crying." There were 46 murdered boys and 37 murdered girls in this sample; 48 were white, 35 were black children.

Nash, John. "The Father in Contemporary Culture and Current Psychological Literature." *Child Development,* June 1973.

Neumann, Charles P. "Health Breakdown May Be Price of Corporate Success Syndrome." *Family Practice News* 5 (January 1975).

Nichols, Beverly. *Father Figure.* New York, Simon and Schuster, 1972.

Ozick, Cynthia. "The Hole Birth Catalog." *Ms.,* 1973.
An excellent article about patriarchy's devaluation of motherhood.

Piercy, Marge. *Living in the Open.* New York: Alfred A. Knopf, 1976.
Read "The Homely War" and those poems contained in the section entitled "The Provocation of the Dream."

Pitchford, Kenneth. *Color Photos of the Atrocities.* Boston: Little, Brown & Co., Atlantic Monthly Press Book, 1973.
A strong and unique collection of poems about being an artist, a human being, a male, feminist, effeminist, faggot, father, lover, husband, and house-husband.

———. "A Triptych of Sonnets." *Double-F: a magazine of effeminism,* no. 3 (Winter, 1975–76).

Pleck, Joseph. "My Male Sex-Role—and Ours." WIN, April 11, 1974.

———. *Resource Guide for the Study of Men.* Bibliography 4th Edition, January 1974. Unpublished; obtainable from author, Ann Arbor, Michigan.

Reed, Evelyn. *Woman's Evolution.* New York: Pathfinder Press, 1975.
Reed, in this massive and fascinating book, suggests that civilization's original taboo was concerned not with incest or female chastity, but with food and cannibalism—specifically, *male* cannibalism.

Reich, Wilhelm. *The Murder of Christ: The Emotional Plague of Mankind.* New York: Noonday Press, 1953.

———. *The Sexual Revolution: Toward a Self-Governing Character Structure.* New York: Farrar, Straus & Giroux, 1969.

———. *The Mass Psychology of Fascism.* New York: Farrar, Straus & Giroux, 1970.

Reik, Theodor. *Ritual: Four Psychoanalytic Studies.* New York: Grove Press, 1946.

Resnick, Phillip J. "Child Murder by Parents: A Psychiatric Review of Filicide." *American Journal of Psychiatry,* September 1969.
The data are highly controversial and incomplete. What is interesting—if true—is the extent to which mothers are seen as committing filicide and/or filicide-suicide out of explicitly "altruistic" motives, and the extent to which fathers are seen to commit filicide due to "psychosis" or to an "unwanted child," due to "accident" or as a means of "spouse revenge." The mothers were hospitalized as lunatic, schizophrenic "Medeas"; the fathers were executed or sent to prison. There is no male equivalent of "Medea" offered to describe the father as child killer.

Rokeach, Milton. *The Three Christs of Ypsilanti.* New York: Alfred A. Knopf, 1964.

Rollman-Branch, Hilda S. "The First-Born Child, Male Vicissitudes of Preoedipal Problems." *International Journal of Psychoanalysis* 47 (1966).
Rollman-Branch notes that just when a sibling arrives, the "privileged" firstborn son "may be severely frustrated, leaving him destructively envious of the mother's (re)productive capacity. Under unfavorable circumstances, both the first-born's ability to work and to love *may be* seriously impaired. Under favorable conditions, his creativity *may be* enhanced and his love relations with women satisfactory."

Rossman, Michael. "Masturbation and Consciousness Raising Groups as Adjunctive Therapy in the Treatment of Male Sexual Dysfunction." Unpublished article, 1975.

Roth, Philip. *Portnoy's Complaint.* New York: Random House, 1967.

Rowe, Mary. "Human Studies Bibliographies." Unpublished, Massachusetts Institute of Technology, Humanities Library.

Ruether, Rosemary Bradford, ed. *Religion and Sexism: Images of Women in the Jewish and Christian Traditions.* New York: Simon and Schuster, 1974.

Sanders, Ed. *The Family.* New York: Avon Books, 1971.
An early account of the Manson murders.

Sarraute, Nathalie. *Tropisms.* Translated by Maria Jolas. New York: George Braziller, 1963.

Schatzman, Morton. *Soul Murder: Persecution in the Family.* New York: Random House, 1973.
A true and well-told tale of extreme father-son persecution and its extreme consequences. It took place in pre-Nazi Germany.

Schnier, Jacques. "Dragon Lady." *American Imago* 4 (1946).
Schnier notes that the "sex of the monster [is crucial]; the hero battles a female of the species . . . no young male [in certain tribes] can be considered a man until he has killed an old woman."

Schwab, Gustav. *Gods and Heroes.* New York: Pantheon Books, 1946.

Seidenberg, Robert. "Oedipus and Male Supremacy." *Radical Therapist,* 1972. A good reinterpretation of the Freudian Oedipus myth in terms of the reality of father power and patriarchy.

Selby, Hubert, Jr. *Last Exit to Brooklyn.* New York: Grove Press, 1964.
An excellent collection of short stories depicting, often too graphically, powerless man's inhumanity to men—and to women.

Shaw, George Bernard. *Pygmalion.* Baltimore: Penguin Books, 1951.

Sheleff, Shaskolsky Leon. "Beyond the Oedipus Complex. A Perspective on the Myth and Reality of Generational Conflict." Unpublished article, Tel-Aviv University, 1974.
Sheleff proposes a "Rustum complex" in lieu of an Oedipus complex. Rustum—as inadvertently as Oedipus—kills his son Sohrab in battle. This is an excellent review of the psychological and mythological literature about fathers and sons and the systematic denial, by organized and/or accepted psychiatric thought, of paternal infanticidal wishes, ambivalence, and hostility.

Slater, Philip E. *The Glory of Hera: Greek Mythology and the Greek Family.* Boston: Beacon Press, 1968.

Smith, Homer W. *Man and His Gods.* New York: Grosset and Dunlap, 1952.

Snodgrass, Jon. "The Women's Liberation Movement and the Men." Paper presented at the Pacific Sociological Association Meetings, Victoria, British Columbia, 1975.

Solanas, Valerie. *SCUM Manifesto.* New York: Olympia Press, 1967.
A fierce, scathing, passionate radical pamphlet.

Solzhenitsyn, Aleksandr I. *The Gulag Archipelago: One and Two.* New York: Harper & Row, 1974, 1976.
A detailed account of powerful and powerless man's inhumanity to man. After reading both volumes, I found myself repeating a line from Wertmuller's film *Seven Beauties:* "Man's only hope lies in disorder."

Sophocles. *Oedipus the King.* Translated by R. C. Jebb. In *Seven Famous Greek Plays.* New York: Random House, 1938, 1950.

———. *Antigone.* Translated by R. C. Jebb. In *Seven Famous Greek Plays.* New York: Random House, 1938, 1950.

Stannard, Una. "The Male Maternal Instinct." *Trans-action,* November-December 1970. Reprinted by KNOW Inc., Pittsburgh, Pennsylvania 15232.

Stanton, Elizabeth Cady, *et al. The Woman's Bible.* Seattle: Seattle Coalition Task Force on Women and Religion, 1974.
A moving, concise, and wonderful theological reinterpretation of the Old and New Testament by early feminists and feminist theologians.

Stern, Karl. *The Flight from Woman.* New York: Noonday Press, Farrar, Straus & Giroux, 1965.

Stoltenberg, John. "Eroticism and Violence in the Father-Son Relationship." In Jon Snodgrass, ed., *For Men Against Sexism: A Book of Readings.* Albion, Calif.: Times Change Press, 1977.

———. "Toward Gender Justice." In Jon Snodgrass, ed., *For Men Against Sexism: A Book of Readings.* Albion, Calif.: Times Change Press, 1977.

Stone, Chuck. "Psychology and the Black Community: From Arthur 1853 to Arthur 1969." Paper presented at the American Psychological Association, September 1971.

"The Male Menopause: For Some, There's a Sense of Panic." *The New York Times,* April 1971.

"There Comes a Will to Live." *The New York Times Magazine,* January 1974.

Tillich, Hannah. *From Time to Time.* New York: Stein and Day, 1973.

Tolstoy, Leo. *The Kreutzer Sonata.* Translated by Isai Kamen. New York: Random House, Vintage Books, 1957.

Tresemer, David, and Pleck, Joseph. *Sex Role Boundaries and Resistance to Sex Role Change.* Vol. 2, *Women's Studies.* New York: Gordon & Breach Science Publications, 1974.

Vanggaard, Thorkil. *Phallos: A Symbol & Its History in the Male World.* New York: International University Press, 1969.

Virgil (Publius Vergilius Maro). *The Aeneid.* Translated by C. Day Lewis. New York: Oxford University Press, 1952.

Watson, Jane Duncan, and Duncan, Glen M. "Murder in the Family: A Study of Some Homicidal Adolescents." *American Journal of Psychiatry,* May 1971.

Parental physical brutality is related to adolescent homicide.

Wellish, Erich. *Isaac and Oedipus: A Study in Biblical Psychology of the Sacrifice of Isaac, the Akedah.* London: Routledge & Kegan Paul, 1954.

Young, Allen. "Some Thoughts on How Gay Men Relate to Women." *After You're Out. Personal Experiences of Gay Men and Lesbian Women.* New York: Links Books, 1976.

Young notes that "it was easier telling women [about being gay] than telling straight men. This is another universal experience of male homosexuals. In our families, too, it is easier to tell our sisters than our brothers, easier to tell our mothers than our fathers. . . . There seems to be a level of [sympathy], of understanding and acceptance of which men are not capable [if their manhood is being threatened]. No wonder, did you ever hear a woman beating up a man because he is a faggot?"

Yourcenar, Marguerite. *Memoirs of Hadrian.* Translated by Grace Frick in collaboration with the author. New York: Farrar, Straus & Giroux, 1963.

BOOKS READ AFTER I COMPLETED THIS ONE

Baraheni, Reza. *The Crowned Cannibals, Writings on Repression in Iran.* With an Introduction by E. L. Doctorow. New York: Random House, Vintage Books, 1977.

This is an excellent and extraordinary book: part indictment of torture and repression in Iran, part personal account of the author's own imprisonment, torture, and exile. There is also an excerpt from Baraheni's book *Masculine History,* in which he recognizes both the oppression of women and the actual and spiritual cannibalism and infanticide practiced by fathers against sons and by father figures against son- and daughter-figures. Let me quote from the book directly:

> . . . one definition of the kings of Iran is that they are youth-killers. Our crowned cannibals find the flesh of young men and women more palatable. Our history is the history of infanticide. Iranian literature is imbued with such striking examples of gerontocracy, infanticide and cannibalism that we can say with certainty that the most important pattern in all the genres of Persian literature is the killing of the young for the preservation of the old. The godhead of all myth, legend and history in Iran is the aged male—the traditional devourer of the youth.
>
> There are no stories surpassing these in the epic literature of the country, and all four of them are stories of fathers killing, or participating in the killing of, their sons and other young men.

> The father as a positive thesis in the literature of Masculine History is so powerful that he rushes headlong toward his antithesis [the son]. . . . Dialectically speaking, the son is crushed under the weight of the father. . . . In this world there are fathers replacing fathers replacing fathers, a tedious succession of men in blood with sleeves tucked up to ravish ages of people.

Dinnerstein, Dorothy. *The Mermaid and the Minotaur: Sexual Arrangements and Human Malaise*. New York: Harper & Row, 1976.
This is a very good account of male and female psychology under patriarchy. Dinnerstein states some of what I do in a more balanced, reasoned, and academic tone, and is careful to "match" each of the minotaur's failings, sins, or dilemmas with one of the mermaid's.

Henley, Nancy. *Body Politics: Sex, Power and Nonverbal Communication*. Englewood Cliffs, N.J.: Prentice-Hall, 1977.
A good academic account of the politics of touching, of male (and female) body language.

Hite, Shere. *The Hite Report*. New York: Macmillan, 1976.
An excellent survey of female sexuality. The "why" of male sexual behavior, as described and inferred in Hite's book, is explored in my essay "Talking to Men About Sex."

Janus, Sam, Bess, Barbara, and Saltus, Carol. *A Sexual Profile of Men in Power*. Englewood Cliffs, N.J.: Prentice-Hall, 1977.
Reza Baraheni's analysis of Iran as a rule by aged Father-cannibals (see Baraheni entry) is not so totally different from the rest of the patriarchal world. For example, Janus, Bess, and Saltus have noted that past and present congressmen, senators and presidents, barring assassination, live longer than most men—having a mean age of seventy-one at death. More important, they note that:

> In Congress, thanks to the seniority system, increasing age means increasing authority and influence; the older men serve on more important committees and make more of the vital decisions than the younger ones. . . .
>
> 90 percent of [U.S.] Congressmen get reelected over and over; they are the "steadies" who rise to a position of authority and run the establishment. It is the rotating 10 percent of freshmen Congressmen who come and go. . . . Despite the intense competitive infighting, these men work within a sort of old boys' network which offers them some security and protection. Congress does provide a sense of stability and a confidence that once seniority is achieved, the chances are one will be around for some time. . . .
>
> It was the freshmen who supported Hays in the Democratic caucus of 1974–1975, while the older members were seeking to divest him of his chairmanships. When the scandal broke, the freshmen on the whole stayed behind Hays much longer than any of the old guard.

McGrady, Mike. *The Kitchen Sink Papers. My Life as a House Husband.* New York: New American Library, Signet, 1976.

A totally honest account of what it's like for a man to take over the daily responsibility of a home and children, and to accept—no, depend upon—money from his female spouse.

Marquez, Gabriel Garcia. *The Autumn of the Patriarch.* New York: Harper & Row, 1975.

In his portrait of a total dictator, Marquez evokes the death-principle that is now at the heart of our nuclear, increasingly advanced technological totalitarian world. This need to own, control, and kill is often described and denounced as a "phallic" impulse by feminists. Here Marquez describes it, magnificently, from the inside; perhaps he would call the impulse "dictatorial"? certainly "patriarchal." Read the novel. Marquez, like few men, smells and abhors the same decay that I do.

Ochs, Carol. *Behind the Sex of God, Toward a New Consciousness—Transcending Matriarchy and Patriarchy.* Boston: Beacon Press, 1977.

This is a carefully and well thought out book about the psychology and ethics of religious history. Interestingly, the author has a similar interpretation of the importance of father-son sacrifice in the Old Testament to the view stated in this book. Let me quote her on Isaac's sacrifice and the meaning of male immortality.

> What do Isaac and Ishmael have in common that Abraham's other sons lack? The surprising answer is that both were nearly put to death by their father. . . . In matriarchy, a direct covenantal relationship between parent and child exists by reason of a blood tie. In Abraham's patriarchy, the father only becomes deeply related to his sons through a blood sacrifice—theirs. . . .
>
> The relationship of father to son exemplified by the father God to his children, Israel, is the continuing theme of the Old Testament. . . . The Bible, in Bakan's terms, "expresses man's effort to extend the boundary of his ego to include his 'seed.' This particular metaphor for semen is interesting in that it not only suggests property and food, but also tends to make the male even more important than the female, as seed is the determining factor of the nature of the plant, with the soil, water, and sun playing only enabling roles.". . .
>
> Two problems confront the patriarchs: How do they feel about their sons; do they acknowledge them as their own? and How do they deal with their own mortality? Can they extend their "ego boundaries" so that they live on through their seed, or do they "buy" immortality at the expense of their children?

Roth, Philip. *My Life as a Man.* New York: Bantam, 1975.

Russell, Diana E. H., and Van de Ven, Nicole. *Crimes Against Women: The Proceedings of the International Tribunal.* Millbrae, Calif.: Les Femmes Press, 1977.
Read this miraculous book about a miraculous event mainly for the testimonies given by women from forty countries, testimonies that are haunting, dreadful, objective, tales of nearly worldwide rape, wife-beating, sterilization, outlawed abortion, torture of political prisoners, prostitution, forced motherhood, persecution of lesbianism, surgical atrocities, and involuntary psychiatric commitment.

Salter, Kenneth W. *The Trial of Inez Garcia.* Berkeley, Calif.: A Justa Publication Book, 1976.
This is the court transcript of Inez Garcia's trial—which ended in her being indicted for killing the man who held her down while another man raped her. One of the prosecution's chief witnesses against Garcia was the rapist himself. Her sentence was five years to life. Men have been shown more compassion and less publicity for killing other men who raped "their" female property, but when the property itself seeks to defend itself or its honor . . . well, that is another matter. Read this, read Yvonne Wanrow's testimony given in the Brussels

Tribunal, read the newspaper accounts of Joanne Little's trial and think again about the meaning of rape, and what happens when women genuinely want to defend themselves.

Smedley, Agnes. *Portraits of Chinese Women in Revolution.* Edited and with an Introduction by Jan MacKinnon and Steve MacKinnon, Afterword by Florence Howe. Old Westbury, N.Y.: The Feminist Press, 1976.

The writing here is spare, sharp, evocative, as good as Jean Rhys. The portraits are of men as well as women.

Snodgrass, Jon. "Four Replies to Radical Feminism: Marxism, Revolutionary Effeminism, Gay Marxism and Men's Liberation." Paper presented in San Diego, March 1976.

———, ed. *For Men Against Sexism: A Book of Readings.* Albion, Calif.: Times Change Press, 1977.

A good anthology of writings by men about themselves, about women, about sexism.

PICTURE CREDITS

Page	Credit
Page 5	UNESCO and the New York Graphic Society, Ltd.
7	Museo del Prado
11	Museum of Fine Arts, Boston
16–17	The Tate Gallery, London
23	Columbia University
31	Musée du Louvre
33	Musée de Cluny
36	Bibliothèque Nationale
38	La Biblioteca Mediceo Laurenziana di Firenze
42	Sistine Chapel, The Vatican
43	The Tate Gallery, London
49	Musée du Louvre
53	Bibliothèque Royale Albert Ier, Brussels
59	Eberhard Kronhausen, Paris
61	The Metropolitan Museum of Art, New York
64	Cambridge University
69	Pitti Palace, Florence
77	Oslo Kommunes Kunstsamlinger, Munch-Museet
81	Museum Boymans van Beuningen, Rotterdam
87	The Trustees, The National Gallery, London
93	Moravian Museum, Brno, Czechoslovakia
101	Diogenes Verlag AG, Zurich
105	Musée du Louvre
110	Kunsthistorischen Museums, Vienna
113	Musée Granet, Aix-en-Provence
114–15	Verlag Walther H. Schunemann, Munich
118	The Metropolitan Museum of Art, New York
123	Museum of Fine Arts, Boston
124–25	Museo del Prado
128	Pitti Palace, Florence
129	Musée du Louvre
133	eeva-inkeri, New York
140, 141	Richard S. Levitt Foundation, Des Moines, Iowa
145	Prints Division, The New York Public Library, Astor, Lenox and Tilden Foundations